A CATALOGUE OF COMMON PEOPLE

by

Mark Darrah

Roots & Branches

Denton, Texas

Roots & Branches
An imprint of AWOC.COM Publishing
P.O. Box 2819
Denton, TX 76202

Manufactured in the United States of America.

ISBN: 978-1-62016-137-1 - Paperback
ISBN: 978-1-62016-145-6 - Ebook

In memory of
CAROLINA B. and DWIGHT D. DARRAH,
my beloved parents.

In appreciation of
DONALD B. DARRAH and JIM F. GASSAWAY,
and the other great raconteurs of my life.

For, as always,
JACKIE,
my alluring wife.

Dedicated to
the
UNCOMMON COMMON PEOPLE
whose stories are told here.

Table of Contents

Catalogues
(An Introduction)

On the prairie, houses still stand that were purchased by mail order from Sears & Roebuck in the late 1890's. Not just windows or doors but whole structures, ordered from the catalogue, were delivered to remote and desolate places by train and wagon. The buildings came unassembled with instructions, similar to the way children's toys arrive at Christmas. The pieces were put together, and a house stood. As the nineteenth century became the twentieth, these homes proved you could buy whatever you wanted so long as you had a Sears & Roebuck catalogue.

The big retailer no longer publishes its wish book. Children no longer look at the bright pages and circle what they want. Pubescent boys don't sneak peeks at the lingerie pages and wonder what those contraptions do and whether women they know actually wear those things. Sears' management must have thought people no longer lived in isolated places, so the need for the all-encompassing catalogue no longer existed. An American tradition died.

Or did it?

What is the internet other than a huge catalogue? Those of the paper variety still arrive by mail, of course, just fewer in number and now more directly targeted to interested customers. By scrolling through the electronic pages or thumbing through the paper ones, you can find, it seems, whatever you might imagine you want in a catalogue.

That is the lure: imagination. Catalogues offer things to buy, but they sell the ethereal. Comfort. Peace. Knowledge. Convenience. Life in Coolville. Prowess. Beauty and pleasure. A more grounded existence.

Catalogues sell the hope of a vibrant life. That's what they really sell.

The better life, though, comes from the within and the without, not from the transitory which rusts and decays. Better life comes from within by illumination. From without, when we observe and learn from the wisdom of others and the world around us.

The following collection of essays and commentaries is a catalogue of a different sort. It's a catalogue of people. Just as we often overlook the beautiful and unusual around us, so, too, do we overlook the wisdom of those present in our own lives.

The folks you will meet in this volume are common. Their names will never be included in history books. None invented or wrote anything life changing. Some names and circumstances have been changed to protect professional confidences and privacy, but the people you will encounter and their stories are quite real. Forgive the author for a few digressions along the way and writing about places and ideas, too.

We are surrounded by the extraordinary.

Mark Darrah
Tulsa, Oklahoma
July, 2015

Never As It Appears
March 2004

Every fall the teachers in my western Oklahoma grade school thumbtacked poster board pictures of bright cornucopias and bushy sheathes of grain on the bulletin boards in our classrooms. We sang happy songs about the harvest. At Thanksgiving, we dressed as Pilgrims and Indians and celebrated the blessings reaped at the end of growing season.

It didn't make any sense.

The flat fields surrounding my town were bare red and dusty except for fenced rangeland where sturdy Herefords chewed gray grass. Everyone knew harvest was at the end of May or the beginning of June, not in October or November like we sang.

The farmers of my childhood grew winter wheat. Planted in the fall, that strange Ukrainian hybrid prospers under December's snow, grows emerald green in winter, and then turns ruddy gold with the heat of summer's dawn.

Friends accuse me of stubborn doubt, but I haven't believed anyone since the days we celebrated harvest when there was no harvest.

Test given truth; find and live your own. That's what the German farmers in western Oklahoma know, even if they won't tell you.

It's spring in my small city huddled next to the wide Arkansas River in the gnarly cross-timbers of eastern Oklahoma. Lawns hint of green and daffodils bloom in backyards. Teen-aged girls wear too-tight t-shirts and the sun feels good against the skin. In the Ozark foothills to the east, redbuds will soon sprout pink, accented by the faint white of blooming dogwoods in the shadows. Creeks run faster, clearer this time of year. The scents of earth and new life suffuse all.

I seek the flat, ugly plains, though, in springtime.

For most people, this expanse is a natural purgatory, a place you have to get through to get somewhere else. For me, it's where sunsets take up half the sky and grains in season rattle against the always-blowing wind. You never feel locked in; the horizon never ends. At night, more stars shine than you can ever count.

Sure, I've tasted the bitter dust blown in my face. I've dodged rattlers in the gypsum hills. I've waited nights in storm shelters as tornadoes dance their destructive tangos all around. I've felt like the ancient mariner on a sea of dry, broken earth with the burning sun never relenting.

But on the plains, I've seen colors in the sky Matisse never imagined. I've touched the delicate stem of a phlox blooming in a bar ditch. I've laughed with the gopher and he at me. I've seen a dozen Santas in one afternoon's clouds. Here I'm immense and insignificant at the same time.

One spring weekend, my wife and I traveled to western Oklahoma. As the lands flattened, purple black clouds whirled and grumbled until they took up most of the sky. Light turned to dark. Water poured from the sky, flooding the lonely road we traveled. I backed the car to higher ground and waited the storm out.

When the rain let up, it was night. The storm had not ended, though; the water had just stopped falling. As we trekked further onto the plains, lightning crackled and thunder boomed, above, behind, in front, and all around us.

Bursts of light lit the hidden architecture of the night clouds. Skeletons of old windmills and broken down farmhouses jumped out from the dark. We saw the cottonwoods weeping over the banks of the Cimarron. Our car vibrated as thunder crashed too close. An electrical carnival made miracles in the black sky and all around us. Beautiful and frightening, sublime and terrorizing, overwhelming and surprising, like life itself.

It's not really spring where I live. Not yet. The temperature will drop one more time to fourteen degrees Fahrenheit and we'll get seven and a half inches of snow, just after we've convinced ourselves the cold weather has passed. Nothing ever is as it appears to be.

If you want to know freedom, leave your boxy villages and go out to the Great Plains. Stretch your arms and feel the sky.

When you doubt there is a God, leave your mountains and your hills. Go to western Oklahoma and hope for a springtime thunderstorm to roll in.

The Ones Who Have Been Set Free
May 14, 1999

My friend, Rosemary, her husband, and another couple went to the mountains of Nevada a few years ago for a Christmas of snow, beautiful scenery, and the incredible outdoors. Instead they got five days inside a too-small cabin, torrential rains, mud slides, and the last flight out of Reno before the city flooded and the airport shut down. At least, Rosemary and her husband did; the other couple didn't do as well. They tried to escape across the flooding deserts of northern Nevada to Salt Lake City, only to become stranded there.

Rosemary says her vacations always include "events." Otherwise, they wouldn't be memorable. The other couple swears if this is true, they will never travel with Rosemary again.

My parents once had a vacation of "events." Summer, 1957. A road trip to California with one son barely four years old, the other not quite one.

I don't like the way my mother always starts the story. It kind of embarrasses me. I like to think of the trip as the one where I learned to walk. My mother, though, always begins: "You were just a baby and you sat on your little potty chair by the side of the road all the way from here to California and back." You can see why I like to think of it as the trip where I learned to walk.

I've gotten kind of used to my mother's beginning of the story, though. My wife now thinks I spend too much time in the bathroom. I'm convinced I'm just waiting for the next semi to pass. In my younger days when I thought I might become famous, I imagined historical markers being put up along old Highway 66 that had an engraved picture of me and that read: "I sat here in my potty chair in 1957." It's probably a good thing I didn't become famous.

By all accounts, the trip was eventful—for reasons other than the unairconditioned car, the stops on the busiest highway in the country, the two small children, and the smelly potty seat. My mother had never met my father's natural mother, Laura, or her third husband, Gilbert. My mother had just lost her father and knew her husband hadn't seen his birth mother in years. That, I think, was part of the motivation for the trip—for my father to try to know his own mother better before it was too late. Of course, I still wonder about the potty chair stops every two or three hours across the Southwest desert.

Dad had tried to explain some things about his family to my mother, but like so much, full appreciation comes only from experience. My grandmother was eccentric—not rich and eccentric, just eccentric. As a young woman, she was quite beautiful. As the youngest member of her family, she had always been treated like a princess. Little Laura, they called her. When she became an adult, her beauty, charm, and passion for fun collided with real world responsibilities.

Laura's first marriage ended on the dry plains of western Oklahoma, the result of a husband probably too young to get married, a suffocating mother-in-law, and the boredom of small town life for a 1920's good-time girl. She lost custody of her only son. Of course, it didn't help that her ex-husband was county judge in the court where the legal battles over the small boy were fought.

Laura's second husband abused her, drank too much, and did not provide the life Laura had expected. That marriage ended with an impersonal phone call from a charity hospital. "Mr. Glass expired at such and so time today." Click. Little Laura. Not too long thereafter, she suffered "a nervous breakdown," as it was gingerly called then. In the mid-1940's, Laura married Gilbert Lopez, a native-born American of Hispanic descent.

As my parents and their two small boys drove into Los Angeles in 1957, my father knew some of what to expect. He remembered not spending too much time with his mother as a boy. His mother's too-tumultuous life—and skills too undeveloped to care for a child—meant my father spent most of his time with other California relatives. My father tried to tell my mother, but some things must be experienced.

Grandma and Grandpa Lopez lived near Beacon Hill in Los Angeles. In those days, Beacon Hill was not a place of affluence and urban redevelopment, but rather a crowded neighborhood of those on the margins living the big city life. The rundown apartment house where Grandma and Grandpa lived appears in every Raymond Chandler novel: "It was an old building; a book of miserable and heart breaking stories read too often and then left too long on the shelf. I was afraid to blow the dust off and walk in, but knew I had no choice."

My mother was shocked. "An event," Rosemary would say.

Grandma no longer appeared to be "Little Laura." Her small frame carried a lot of extra weight. Her beauty robbed by a hard life and age, she desperately tried to preserve it with too much make-up and too much bleach. She wore bold colors and spoke in monologues. She loved good food and drink. She smoked like a 1949 Roadster without a muffler in city traffic. Charming, demanding, and vulnerable all at once. In a word, Grandma was eccentric.

Grandpa Lopez—Librado as my grandmother called him—wore his dark good looks and gracious charm like a tailored suit. He was so happy... He was so delighted... He was so pleased... He loved the children. He taught me to walk.

Grandma and Grandpa had arranged for us to stay in a vacant apartment there on Beacon Hill. It was so unkempt and dirty, it shocked my mother. Yet, it was a gracious act. What could they do? Then my father became ill, deathly ill. Grandma and Grandpa had no doctor and knew of no doctors. When my father had a vision of his late father-in-law calling him to the other side, my mother wondered what she would do: Two small children and a dying husband in a strange, big city. And, strange in Los Angeles does not mean unfamiliar as it might in other big cities. It means literally what it says: Strange. Fortunately, someone had the insight to call my practical, Norwegian Aunt Louise. She knew someone to call. My father recovered.

"An event" Rosemary would call it. An eventful trip by anyone's standards: Meeting my unique grandmother and her charming husband. Staying in a dilapidated apartment house. My father almost dying. Me taking my first step. Yet, my mother still begins the story by saying, "You were just a baby and you sat on your little potty chair by the side of the road all the way from here to California and back..."

There were two other trips to California that will make this story complete. Nine years later, we went back to California. This time with my younger sister. Grandma and Grandpa had moved. Another Raymond Chandler apartment house in another crowded neighbor of those who live on the margins. Yet, by the lives they led, you would not have known. Grandma held court and we were her royal audience. Grandpa waited on her as if she were royalty. He still loved the children. Every time we came, he went to the pop machine and bought us ice-cold sodas. What child doesn't like a cold Coke? By the last day, though, I didn't think I could drink another. Yet, the act was so gracious, what could I do?

The next trip wasn't as pleasant. 1971. Grandma had died. Mom and Dad travelled to Los Angeles alone. They arranged the funeral and bought the plot. My grandfather—Grandmother's Librado—could only lie in bed naked, drinking wine, and weeping. He had lost his princess. Mom and Dad went through Grandmother's things and found every cent they had ever sent her. New gifts had been crammed into closets and never used. They settled Grandma's affairs, but one remained: Librado. He couldn't stay there like that. What would they do? He had relatives somewhere in Southern California, but my mom and dad had no names and no numbers. My mother got the telephone book and turned to the first page which listed the name "Lopez" and began calling—a task somewhat akin to calling every "Smith" in Chicago. Despite the absurdity of the task—or perhaps because of it—my mother found Gilbert's sister and made arrangements for Gilbert to live there.

The story is still not complete. My brother and I visited Grandfather Lopez eight years later at his sister's home in El Monte. He still wore his charm and graciousness like a well-tailored suit. He reminisced about his days as a street car conductor in the San Gabriel Valley. Although he was over eighty years old, he could still call out the names of every town the streetcar went through. He told us he walked five miles a day. Often, he would take the bus to Santa Monica beach and walk there—the sun and the spray of the ocean in his face.

He showed us a colored drawing: Pretty Laura and Handsome Librado forever frozen in their lives of the 1940's. He talked about how much he missed his "wife and best friend." What best friend did he lose, too? I wondered. He meant his wife, my grandmother.

Then he told us this story: "In the 1920's, everyone told me 'Gilbert, save your money, put your money in the bank.' I didn't. I had a good time. 1929 came around. They had no money. I had no money, but I had had a good time."

We lost track of Grandpa Lopez when he was about 90 years old. He was still walking five miles a day. He was still kind and gracious. I would like to think he is still walking the beaches, that he still loves children, that he still wears his charm and graciousness like a well-tailored suit, but he would be well over 100 now. Perhaps somewhere and somehow he is.

When my brother and I saw him in 1979, I asked him how it was that he married my grandmother. Grandpa explained he met her when she worked at the downtown LA Library. "I had a choice of marrying your grandmother or another woman," he said. "Your grandmother needed me more so I married her."

Librado is an uncommon name. How it was that Gilbert became Librado or Librado became Gilbert is not known. Librado literally means "the one who has been set free." I like to think that when my grandmother found someone who would treat her like a princess and my grandfather found someone he could love, they were both set free.

My grandfather helped me take my first step. There are more important things he taught: To be gracious and kind to a fault; to call your spouse your "best friend" and mean it; to love with such passion you are willing to let your heart break; and when the next 1929 comes, to make sure you have had fun.

There is another element of this story to make it complete and it is what my mother teaches. When the events of life seem overwhelming, remember the blessings of the absurd—like calling every Lopez in the LA phone book or seeing the image of a toddler on a potty seat by the side of the road in the hot Arizona sun, waiting for the next semi to pass.

Monuments
May 2008

When I die, I don't want to be cremated, burned, or fried. I don't want my ashes in an urn, in a little box, or spread over the ocean.

I want to be buried.

It's cheaper to be cremated, I know, more ecologically sound. I'll be just as dead. Ashes to ashes, dust to dust; it's all the same. I'm not concerned about missing the blowing of a trumpet on judgment day. If there really is one, the same God who could bring life to dry bones could bring life to ashes.

I want to be buried, and not at a cemetery where the gravestones have to be flush with the ground so it's easier to mow the grass. The family plot at the Cottonwood Cemetery at Hitchcock, Oklahoma would be just fine. A wooden box and a few bars of "The Streets of Laredo" as they drop me in the hole would be just fine. Maybe a short prayer or a few jokes, too.

Bury me in a place where the tombstones are different sizes, different shapes, and tell different stories.

You see, that is why I want to be buried.

The companies that sell grave markers are never called "Smith Gravestone Company" or "Jones Tombstone Store." They are always called "Monument" companies. That is really what a grave and its marker are: A monument to life, a monument to death, and a monument to the eternity of the life that was.

The monuments—the ones of different sizes, shapes, and colors, not the rock file cards flush to the ground— tell stories of life. Some read "Father," "Wife," "Sister," or "Brother." Some have poems inscribed. Some have pictures engraved or scenes portrayed. I've even seen one with Minnie Mouse on it. My nephew's is shaped as a burning flame.

I want mine to read: "Friend of the Cleaning People." This is why:

When I went to college in California, I lived in a university-owned apartment house maintained by three housekeepers: Bessie, Benny, and Lily.

Now Lily was cool. She was a African-American lady about 60 years old. A single man named Dan managed the residence. One afternoon, as was his custom, Dan entertained a young woman in his apartment. Meanwhile, another woman Dan was seeing walked into the apartment house lobby where Lily was sweeping. This second female visitor asked where she might find Dan's apartment. Like I said, Lily was cool. She replied, "Mister Dan isn't here right now. I don't know where he went or when he will be back, but if you tell me who you are, I'll tell him you stopped by." I figure Lily saved Dan's life that afternoon.

Every week, Benny, Bessie, and Lily cleaned every apartment in the building. It was a luxury, but probably a wise decision by the college administration. One hundred and twenty single freshmen would have otherwise turned the place into a wasteland. The three housekeepers worked with good energy and little complaint: vacuuming and mopping the apartment floors, scrubbing the bathroom fixtures, disposing of items growing blue hair in the kitchen, and emptying the trash.

One late winter afternoon, Lily moved slower than usual as she pushed the Hoover sweeper over the avocado-colored carpet. Her each action unusually labored. I invited her to sit down and share a Coke with me. She accepted, and we talked.

"California's a little different than Oklahoma, I imagine," she said.

"Yes, ma'am," I replied.

"How do you like it here?" Lily asked.

From the kitchen table where we sat, I could see the brown smog haze hovering over the LA skyline.

"I like it just fine," I said. "There's a lot of stuff to do I'd never get to back home, but no one out here seems to know how to fry chicken. I miss real home cooking. I certainly do that."

We made more small talk and finished our Cokes. Lily went back to work, and I thought nothing more about it.

Two months later, someone knocked at the door. It was Lily.

She said, "You know, Benny, Bessie, and I have a little kitchen in the basement they let us use. We'd like for you to come down and have lunch with us tomorrow."

I accepted and when I went to the kitchen basement the next day, Lily had fixed a feast. It was the first real home cooked meal I had had in months and Lily knew how to fix fried chicken.

Now I've have made it a habit of working late at the office and that means it's not unusual for the cleaning crew to arrive before I leave. I always try to be kind to the cleaning people.

I remember Lily.

Celebrate! Cook!
November 2003

In Laura Esquivel's novel *Like Water For Chocolate*, Tita, a young Mexican woman, loves to cook and her emotions flow into the food she prepares. If Tita is sad, those who eat her cooking cry. If happy, those who eat her food laugh. In one scene, Tita lusts after a handsome young man as she fixes a meal. In the next, her sister eats two or three bites of Tita's cooking, rips off all her clothes, and chases down her lover.

Perhaps there is some truth in this story. Have you ever eaten a meal prepared by someone who thinks cooking is a chore, rather than a joy? The meal usually tastes like it's a chore. I mean, has a Big Mac ever made you want to get naked? A meal prepared by someone who delights in it usually is a delight. When I make chocolate chip cookies, I listen to Elvis. If you feel a little snap after you eat something I bake, you now know why.

Sometimes it depends on the emotion the eater brings to the meal. Business lunches, for example. I don't like business lunches or, for that matter, business dinners, because whether eaten at a five-star restaurant or at Big Bertha's Diner, the result is the same. The food isn't tasted. It isn't celebrated. You might as well be eating cardboard.

I like to cook. I used to think it was because my father and I cooked together when I was a kid. Christmas candy, primarily. Divinity, fudge, and especially peanut brittle. We'd wait by the stove for the sugary syrup to reach the right temperature, mix in the peanuts, wait for the stuff to turn to a pale reddish brown, mix in the soda and vanilla. And then: Voila! Christmas peanut brittle!

There are some of Dad's cooking concoctions and habits I still know and have. The "Oh Drat!" waffle, for example. That's the one that burns and sticks to the sides of the griddle. You say "Oh drat!" when you have to scrape it out with a knife.

I've learned, too, why our dogs always got a pancake or two when Dad fixed them. Almost invariably Dad would say "This pancake's for Shawn (or Heinrich, or Poodles, depending on which dog was living at our house at that time)." I now know why now. If the griddle's not hot enough when you pour the batter, the first pancake just doesn't come out very good. That's the dog's pancake. When I drop something on the floor while cooking, I turn and look for a dog to come eat what has landed, even though I don't own a dog. When there are leftover beaten eggs and milk for French toast, I think I have to find an animal to give it to. These are Dad cooking habits. I don't intend to lose them and probably never will.

My mother, though, really taught me to cook. I don't remember much of any particular lesson. Mom's instruction was here and there: a suggestion, a comment, a "let me show you." One lesson came by long distance when she taught me how to fry chicken. I lived in Southern California then and loved college life there, except no one knew how to fry chicken like Mama. She taught me by telephone. It didn't come out as bad as you might think.

Does every son think his mother is the best cook in the world? Most maybe, but not all. My mother was and is.

She'd drive us nuts on holidays. All morning, all evening, in the middle of the night, she cooked: Candies, cookies, and these awesome meals.

My sister and my brother are both creative. My sister paints and draws wonderful pictures. She takes little things and makes incredible big works of art out of them. My brother uses a camera and makes fascinating images of color, lines, and light. I enjoy writing. My mother wonders why her children like to create.

The answer is in the scents and tastes of those holiday meals. You see, my mother put her emotion into her cooking long before *Like Water for Chocolate* was ever written. After opening packages or watching the Thanksgiving parade, Mama would bring out an amazing and huge meal: salads, two or three vegetables, casseroles, meats, breads, desserts, drinks. Mama would present this wonderful creation!

That's what cooking is: a creation.

And eating?

A celebration of that creation and of the good earth's abundance.

An Unacknowledged Zen Master
December 1997

For most of the time I was in law school, my father worked as a district superintendent for the United Methodist Church. If the Methodist Church of the 1980's were to be compared to today's Pizza Hut, he would have been called a regional team leader, the guy you called if the minister ran off with the Sunday morning collection or the local barmaid. Dad traveled from congregation to congregation to show his support and to be of help, but I'm sure his unannounced presence rattled some of his younger, more inexperienced ministers. I didn't attend church much back then, and I knew it would have pleased my parents if I had.

One Saturday, Dad called.

"I'm preaching in Purcell tomorrow," he said. "Why don't you come?"

Purcell is about twenty miles down the road from Norman where I lived. Dad rarely confronted my absence from church so directly. He knew my decision and either respected it or was resigned to it.

"OK," I said, with not much enthusiasm.

"Now, it's not the big church where I'm preaching; it's the smaller one."

"Where is it?"

"Are you familiar with Purcell?" he asked.

"Not really."

"Well, it's in the southeast part of town. The streets aren't marked. You'll get lost and then you'll find it."

I should have known by then that when my father said something like this, I would learn no more, but still I asked:

"What do you mean?"

"I don't know how else to tell you. You'll get lost and then you'll find it."

The next morning I drove to Purcell and found the southeast part of town. Dad was right. The streets weren't marked. Then, I got lost and just about when I had given up and decided to try to find my way back to Norman, I turned the corner and saw a white frame building that, judging by the cars and the appearance, was a Methodist church. Were all small town Oklahoma Methodist churches designed by the same architect? Although no sign designated its denomination, I knew. This was the smaller of the Methodist churches in Purcell. I had no doubt Dad would be speaking here soon.

I parked the car and walked through the front door and into the sanctuary. Everyone in the room turned and looked at me. I looked at them. Every face was a beautiful black or chocolate or mocha. I looked at my hands. I didn't need a mirror to know my face was the pasty pale of a casebook-reading law student. Mom and Dad were not present. Not anywhere. I had arrived at the church three minutes before the time Dad had told me the service started. My father was never late. I was really lost.

I kind of stuttered and stammered.

A black man at the front of the sanctuary said, "May I help you?"

"My father was supposed to preach..."

"Are you Brother Darrah's son?"

I nodded.

"Have a seat. We're just finishing up Sunday School. I'm sure your folks will be here in a little while."

They were. I don't remember whether Dad gave me the wrong time or whether Mom was running late—both are real possibilities. But they did arrive and Dad preached.

My father spoke that morning about the dangers of reducing people to caricatures by the use of words and labels, but I don't remember what else he said exactly. I haven't forgotten, though, the directions to that church. You see, the longer I live, the more convinced I become that, more often than not, you'll get lost before you find it, and often you have to get lost before you can even figure out what you're looking for.

That morning, the church ladies in their spring-flower hats said "Amen!" like God's own angels, and through the sermon, the men called out "Tell us, Brother! Tell it like it is!" I don't know, though, if they really knew to whom they were listening:

My father, an unacknowledged Zen master.

Sherds and Flakes
November 2008

Here the high desert sun sears in mid-August. My wife and I wear long sleeves and straw hats. We kneel on red earth packed solid by centuries of heat, wind, gushing rain, and solitude. A square-cut hole lies before us. We take our trowels and scrape the solid ground within that square. The cut is neither large nor deep—a little over a yard square and about five inches in depth. Jackie and I move our trowels gently, but the earth and its substance screech in offense.

We feel the sun on our skin; it casts hues of gold and gray. Despite the mountain altitude, I breathe free and full. From time to time, a slight wind breezes through nearby piñon and juniper trees. I smell the sharp blue scent of sage. Jackie takes her hand broom and whisks away some dirt. I taste its pungent red dust as it settles into the air. Other learners kneel and scrape over their own assigned squares of land. Hours pass here without the whistle of birds or the rattle of tree limbs. This place, so remote and so silent.

It wasn't always.

Eight hundred to a thousand years ago, people lived near this very spot, now called Pinyon Place, a part of Hovenweep National Monument. We are in the desert country of southwestern Colorado. Twenty-first century people ranch and dry farm nearby and welcome tourists during the summer. At the Ute Mountain Casino, guests from the Four Corner region drop their dollars into noisy machines. The population here in Montezuma County totals close to twenty-five thousand, about the same as it was eight hundred years ago.

"Drink water! Cool off in the shade!" Becky Hammond yells at us. Our Mountain Ute Educator speaks blunt truth in tones of humor and practical wisdom. "Don't get too hot. You get sick."

We respect her direction, but are eager to search and find. Our quest draws us as gamblers to a jackpot, as prospectors to gold.

Ten to fifteen miles southeast of the place where Jackie and I kneel in the dirt, tourists view the majestic cliff dwellings of Mesa Verde National Park. A few hundred yards to the east, the remains of the Goodman Point Pueblo lay buried—a contemporary community of Mesa Verde, but larger and shorter lasting and built majestically not in cliffs but on the bluffs of a canyon cut by clear stream water. The People who built Mesa Verde and Goodman Point Pueblo are commonly known as the Anasazi. The preferred nomenclature today is Ancestral Puebloans. I think of them simply as The People.

Jackie and I take the loosened earth and dump it into a galvanized bucket. The process takes time. The earth is stubborn and holds its bounty closely. Centuries have passed since human hands touched here.

The People settled in the Mesa Verde Region and began dry farming corn and beans just after the time of Christ. They lived in family communities dispersed over the arid landscape. As time passed, larger settlements developed, although some families remained separate. The People developed skills as superb potters and prosperous farmers. They built masonry structures, dwellings we call pueblos today. About 1150 A.D., The People started congregating in large towns such as Mesa Verde and Goodman Point Pueblo, and just as quickly a century and a half later, The People abandoned the area. By 1300 A.D., the population of Montezuma County dropped from approximately 25,000 to virtually zero.

No one knows why The People suddenly congregated in their defensive pueblo cities or why they abruptly left.

Jackie and I dig at the site of one of the dispersed family communities to assist with research being conducted by the Crow Canyon Archaeological Center of Cortez, Colorado. What the archeologists discover here may help explain why The People congregated en masse at the Goodman Point Pueblo. It may lead to other unexpected insights. We do not know. We scrape the earth and put what we find in the bucket.

Jackie and I are not archeologists. Neither are our fellow learners—Steve, a retired Air Force Colonel from Colorado Springs; Sarah, a student from San Francisco; Susan, a pharmacist from Las Cruces, New Mexico; and Leslie, a young Ivy League grad now living in Napa, California. This week the passionate staff at Crow Canyon have taught us about The People, their artifacts, and how the dates of prehistoric relics are determined. We tour the ruins of the ancient ones. We work in the Crow Canyon lab and learn to make meaning of the unearthed findings. We excavate here in the high desert under the burning sun amid the piñon, juniper, and sage.

Leslie talks and says she's a Cher knockout on karaoke.

"Sing 'Gypsies, Tramps, and Thieves,'" I call out.

"I don't do songs recorded before I was born," she replies.

I scrape up dirt and dump it in the bucket. The artifacts buried here date from the time of King Richard the Lionhearted.

"Let's see what you've found," says Grant Coffey, the supervising field archeologist for this portion of the excavation. I pick up the bucket and walk to a tripod that holds a swinging metal screen. I pour the dirt onto the screen.

The Four Corners area holds the largest collection of prehistoric archeological sites in the country. It numbers in the thousands, perhaps even the ten thousands. The underground family ruin where we work had been located by geographic signs such as piles of rubble rock and unnatural indentions in the land. Its presence had been confirmed by sophisticated electronic scan. A block of pueblo rooms had stood at the north side of this site. Adjacent to the south of it, a kiva—a subterranean family/ceremonial place—lies hidden under the earth and immediately south of that, the midden. That is where we work: in the midden, in the family junk pile, the place where the discards had been thrown eight hundred to a thousand years ago. We are the National Enquirer reporters of ancient times.

I shake the screen and the loose dirt sifts through, leaving stones and pieces of broken pottery. Jackie and Grant join me to pick through what remains on the screen.

Jackie picks up a piece of large corrugated pottery, most probably a part of a cooking vessel.

The stones to retain for examination pose a bigger challenge. We look for ones that have been chipped. Those jagged edges show they have been used as tools or in making tools. The archeologists call them flakes; the broken pieces of pottery, sherds—an abbreviation of the word "potsherd."

I pick up a rock and hand it to Grant. He looks at it. "You've found a pretty piece of sandstone," he says, breaks the stone with his fingers, and tosses it aside. Grant has said this hundreds of times to other novice archeologists, but he speaks the phrase as if it's his first time. His father is a farmer north of here. Grant himself demonstrates the patience of that occupation and of the best teachers.

Jackie finds a piece of red pottery painted with black designs.

"A trade good from over in Utah," Grant says. "Made probably about fifty miles or so west of here." Our lab instructor, Ben Bellorado, had compared the red pottery to the good china brought for use on special holidays.

Jackie holds a part of a Christmas platter from almost ten centuries ago.

She places the sherd in a paper sack that holds the artifacts for this layer of earth within our cut square. When we dig fifteen centimeters, the sack is marked and sealed and another one marked for the artifacts found in the next fifteen centimeters of dirt. Jackie becomes adept at finding the chipped stones, the flakes in even the smallest rocks.

I find a white sherd with a black lightning mark on its inside curve. A piece of Mesa Verde pottery, probably a serving bowl since the design is painted on the sherd's inside curve. Markings on the outside would indicate a jar or storage container. We place dozens of these artifacts into our paper bag.

And on it goes. We scrape the land, fill the bucket, sift the dirt, and search for sherds and flakes, the broken and discarded pieces of the past.

Becky Hammond helps us later. She picks up a stone from the screen and says, "Archeologists date flakes."

Before I got married, I did too, a number of times I think, before I realize she means they determine the age of the chipped rock back in the lab.

Crow Canyon leads in the practice of conservation archeology. This site will not be entirely unearthed. The location of the square cuts where we novice archeologists unearth the midden had been determined at random. The square cut over the kiva where our interns, Dona and Sara, dig had been selected by the archeologists' best estimate of where significant findings would be located. When the artifacts in the square cuts in the midden are exhausted, the square holes will be filled in with the rocks and dirt removed, and the ruin left otherwise undisturbed for other generations of archeologists with more advanced technology and new knowledge to study. Back in the lab, the sherds and flakes will be cleaned, identified, catalogued, and the findings entered into a comprehensive database from which conclusions will be drawn and theories extrapolated. The relics themselves will later be stored at the Anasazi Heritage Center in Delores, Colorado. In our time in the desert, Jackie and I excavate five to seven inches of dirt from a hole about a yard square. We fill one and a half paper lunch bags of sherds and flakes, a tiny, tiny contribution to the knowledge of the ways of the bygone People.

Towards the end of our time of excavation, we uncover the rounded edge of a thick piece of gray corrugated pottery. This is our find. A whole vessel perhaps. Alas, it is not, but when we extricate the sherd from the grip of the land and brush off the dirt, this is what we see:

The fingerprint of the potter pressed on the lip of the broken vessel.

~~~

The trip back home to Tulsa takes longer than the trip going to Cortez. It always takes longer to return than to go. We drive miles over the desert, through the mountains, and then onto the High Plains. I wonder about the value of our endeavor, our hours uncovering the broken and discarded pieces of a time past, our bag and a half of discarded pottery and stone. When we cross into Oklahoma, I begin to see places of remembrance: The turn off to Altus where we lived that one high school year. The rest stop where I waited with my shaggy dog and a broken down car while my roly-poly father hitchhiked up the road for help. The bright prairie woods near the town where I was born.

~~~

I remember the forgotten: the way my mother used to sing a tune known only to her while the car radio played something entirely different, the smell of my grandmother's house when she fixed Thanksgiving dinner, the photograph of my best friend in his uncomfortable suit the day he was named a Presidential Scholar at his college, the way my wife stared the first time we met.

The miles trek on.

Maybe it's not the big moments that make a life. Maybe it's the little, broken pieces, discarded and forgotten, that do. The sherds and flakes of our own existence. And perhaps if we're lucky, we leave a fingerprint that remains a thousand years.

Mister Pence's Texaco Station
September 2004

The new car salesman jacked up the price between the time he made the offer and four weeks later when I had the money and financing to buy. I should have told him to find some integrity and bought elsewhere, but I liked and wanted the car too much.

Thirteen thousand miles later, my new 1977 VW Rabbit collapsed. The engine dismantled, parts ordered from Germany, and three months in the shop. When my father and I redeemed it from the mechanic, I was told to always buy good gasoline and to put an additive like STP in the tank every once in a while.

From then on, I was very careful what kind of gas I put in Harvey. (It was a big, white Rabbit who went everywhere with me, although Elwood P. Dowd was better served.) If Harvey wasn't fed good fuel, he would gasp, cough, sputter, and sometimes just refuse to go. If fed the right stuff, he purred and hopped. To be safe, I put a bottle of STP in the tank every time I purchased gasoline from an unknown vendor.

A small Texaco station stood at the corner of Boyd and Classen in Norman, Oklahoma when I started attending graduate school in the late seventies. Built in the 1920's or 1930's with a faux-Spanish design, the gas station had a driveway that crossed diagonally and big plate glass windows. Only about two or three cars could be serviced there at any one time without others backing up in the drive. I had my father's Texaco card and the station was convenient so I took Harvey there my first week of classes for a fill-up.

The service station attendant worked alone. He wore a uniform which looked as if it had started the day clean and pressed, but now was smudged with work. He checked under the hood, cleaned the windshield, and topped off the tank. When I got ready to pay, I asked if he had any STP or anything that would keep the engine clean. He looked at me as if I had insulted his mother.

"Come here," he said and led me to the gas pump where he brushed the dust off of a little white sticker. "The Corporation Commission came by last week and tested the gas." He pointed to some numbers. "This is the highest rating they give. I sell good gasoline. You don't need STP or any stuff like that when you buy here."

The service station attendant was Mister Pence, the owner. When I drove Harvey away from there, he purred and hopped. Mister Pence was right. The car didn't need STP or anything else when I bought there. It became a habit, the only place I'd fill-up Harvey.

Mister Pence's Texaco Station wasn't flashy or new, but always tidy and clean. There were no other employees, just Mister Pence. He always checked under the hood, showed me the oil mark on the dipstick, cleaned the windows, and topped off the tank. Each day started for him with a clean uniform. As did other men of his generation, he wore his dark hair cut short with a neat part and kept in place with Brylcream or something like it. He wasn't flamboyant, but quiet, calm, and deliberate. The advertising executive who came up with the jingle "You Can Trust You Car To The Man Who Wears the Star" must have been inspired by a visit to Mister Pence's Texaco Station.

When I'd take Harvey for a fill-up, Mister Pence and I would talk about the weather, the headlines, the fortunes of the Sooner football team. He would ask about my classes, about school. I don't remember him ever telling me not to get discouraged or not to give up, but by the way he would ask, I knew that's what he wanted me to hear. He showed the same courtesy and respect to this long-haired temporary college student as he would have the local banker or priest.

One day, I pulled into the station and a little white sign was taped to the door: Closed Temporarily.

Several weeks passed and the station had not reopened. I went to the liquor store next door and asked if they knew what was going on.

"Not sure," the clerk said. "I heard he went into the hospital for some tests, thinking it'd be just a few days. Think they found cancer."

Mister Pence's Texaco Station never opened again.

A new convenience store now stands on that corner. I've never been in it, but I'm sure the folks there are friendly. They'll want to know whether you want some chocolate milk to go with your gasoline or a Hostess Ding Dong with your quart of oil. They'll let you buy all the STP or other fuel additives you want and they'll let you pour whatever you want in your tank. To those folks, though, I'd be just another middle-aged businessman pumping gas and signing a credit card receipt.

Today I have my own law practice. Each morning I get up and put on a clean pressed white shirt, a tie, and a suit. My uniform. I know every client by name and disposition. I try to show the poorest the same respect and courtesy I do the richest.

I can handle about two or three major cases, crises, or transactions at any one time without other work backing up. I am my only employee. Sometimes it's pretty quiet.

My office isn't in a new building and doesn't have a prestigious address. It's a small place, not flashy or new and never quite as tidy as I would like. There's no sticker on the front door certifying the quality of what I do, but I am not ashamed to tell you:

I sell good gasoline.

Always Choose The Bass Boat
August 2007

"Now she was a cool little old lady," Bill Cosby once said, "you see, that's the only way you get to be a little old lady—by being a cool little old lady."

~~~

Margaret's only relatives lived in Maine and Indiana. They never called, never wrote. Margaret had no husband, no children, and no living brothers and sisters.

Why leave one's earthly belongings to people whose only connection to you are common ancestors, particularly when those same people can't punch a few buttons on a telephone?

Margaret decided to give her estate to her friends and to her church.

If not properly signed and witnessed, a will may be successfully contested. Margaret's relatives would certainly find the wherewithal to punch the buttons on a telephone to call an attorney if anything about Aunt Margaret's will looked suspect, particularly if that meant hitting the jackpot and collecting from a deceased aunt's estate.

Margaret had white hair that looked like spun silver. Every time she came to see her lawyer she wore a different navy suit, each the type one wears when one means business. She had been a young housewife when the Great Depression came. By the start of World War II, she had become a widow, never remarrying. When she laughed, you wanted to laugh with her.

Her attorney checked every word in her will twice. He lined up three people to witness her will, although only two are required. He very carefully led Margaret, the witnesses, and the notary through the procedure Oklahoma law requires for the execution of a will.

After completing the ceremony, the attorney led Margaret from his conference room to his office to discuss where to keep her will, how to change it, and to discuss any other questions Margaret may have had.

Margaret sat down and gasped, "I'm breathless!"

Had Margaret waited to die until just the moment her will was finished? Maybe she was just having a spell, but that might require the will to be signed and witnessed again. If she had a spell she never came out of, questions certainly would be raised about the will's validity.

"What's wrong?" her attorney asked. "Is there anything I can do?"

"My brassiere is just too tight," Margaret said.

~~~

Leah lived life with a missionary's zeal to help and protect those hurting and injured. She loved good food, a pleasant night on the town, and company.

In the eighth decade of her life, Leah walked with a walker; each step, a stumble and a push. Leah and her husband, Hubert, invited my wife, Jackie, and I out to dinner at one of my city's exclusive private clubs.

I was thirty-two years old.

Before the walker, before the arthritis, it might have taken Leah five minutes to get from her car to the front door of the nightclub. That evening, it took between ten and fifteen.

As dinner with Hubert and Leah concluded and the dessert dishes were carried away, a dance band began to play. Hubert asked Jackie to dance, and they did. An eighty-five year old man dancing with my wife!

Leah looked at them as they moved over the shining parquet floor.

"Hubert loves to dance, but I can't anymore," Leah said. She took my hand. "Yesterday I was your age."

~~~

Zoe was eighty-one years old when she moved from suburban Seattle to Oklahoma. She had never lived outside her native Northwest and felt like she had moved to Dodge City when she got to Tulsa. Her daughters lived here and wanted to be able to help her in her final years. Her son, a resident of Oklahoma's Little Dixie, would have loved to have had her stay with him. Tulsa was a big enough adjustment.

When she was eighty-nine, Zoe discovered a lump in her breast and she was hospitalized for a radical mastectomy. Surgery was performed, but the wrong breast excised. When she regained consciousness, her surgeon stood by her bed. He explained what had happened and apologized for his gross error.

"Well, Doctor," Zoe said, "I guess my bikini wearing days are over."

~~~

Beatrice was born in Oklahoma's No Man's Land a few months after our state was admitted to the Union. She had outlived her husband by more than a decade.

As Beatrice approached her one hundredth year, she hired me to meet with her and her two children to explain to them how she wanted her final affairs handled and her estate distributed. A gentle woman with skin that looked like wrinkled alabaster, Beatrice had no patience for nonsense and wanted none after she was gone.

Her son had flown into town from Chicago. He had retired a number of years before from a Fortune 500 company, but not before rising to its upper management and wealth beyond most people's imagination.

Beatrice's daughter lived near her mother and had recently ended her work as a human resources manager at a local manufacturing company.

Beatrice, her son and daughter, and I sat down around a table in my conference room. I did what Beatrice had asked me to: explain how she wanted her affairs handled and her estate distributed. And, that she wanted no nonsense.

Beatrice remained after her son and daughter left.

"Did you notice the look on my son's face when you were speaking?" she asked. "Today was the first time he had ever considered my mortality."

~~~

Bob was Hazel's second husband. Like many men, he liked to build things with his hands, and he liked to fish. When Bob retired after years of hard work, he and Hazel had a choice. Bob wanted to build another room onto their house. Hazel wanted to buy a bass boat.

They bought the bass boat and just about every day they could for the following year, they went fishing.

Then Bob had a stroke.

For the next eight years, Bob lived in a nursing home, unable to care for even his most basic needs.

Now Bob has passed on to the other side, and Hazel says this:

"If Bob had started building that room onto the house, it wouldn't have gotten finished before he had his stroke. He would have never gotten to enjoy it. We had so much fun with that bass boat, the two of us. That time together, I'd never trade. So, if you have a choice between buying a bass boat and building a room onto your house, always choose the bass boat."

~~~

Bonita Jane lives alone in a white wooden house on forty acres of farmland in Okfuskee County. Her husband, Buddy, has been gone for the last eight years. Until his last day of life, he wondered why he had survived the Battle of the Bulge when so many good men had perished.

Bonita Jane has never been over five feet tall and as the years pass, she seems to shrink. Her eyes shine as clear as a teenager's. She has never had a broken bone, and she's never taken any prescription medications. Her skin is the color of fresh cut lumber with about as many narrow little lines. Bonita Jane remembers picking cotton when she was eight years old with her sharecropper parents. She won't forget how hot the sun shone on them and that river bottomland.

"I am the only one of my family still living," she tells me. "My husband and my only son are gone. My parents died so many years ago. My sister, my older brother, and now my younger brother—my best friend—have all passed on.

"The next time your family gets together for Thanksgiving or Christmas or for any reason at all, look around the table and remember that someday there will be only one of you remaining."

A Sound Gazetteer
August 2006

I fell in love once because of a woman's voice and a question about a car.

Willie Nelson had celebrated his birthday by playing a concert at Barnhill Arena in Fayetteville, Arkansas until the early hours of the morning. He was ancient, we thought. He had turned forty-four that day. We left before Willie quit singing.

Six of us—male and female college students—packed into a 1970's boat car to look for some ice cream, a coke, and maybe bottled beer and a good time. A nighttime rain fell, but soon stopped. The kid driving laughed and joked as good as any stand-up comedian, but paid little attention to the mechanics. The windshield wipers flapped uselessly across the dry windshield block after block after block.

Debbie asked the question. Her friends called her "Little Debbie" because she was petite and cute, not because her picture appeared on boxes of cookies.

"Why are the windshield wipers on?" Little Debbie asked. I can't write like she spoke it, but if you're from the South, you know how she sounded. When I heard Debbie's question, I fell in love.

Our accent tells people where we are from. In our part of the country, people speak with distinctive cadence, rhythm, and sound, not all necessarily the same, but each a sign of our unique place of belonging. In some of our voices, you can hear an accent as rich as the burnt candy taste of bourbon on a humid Mississippi night. Others have an Ozark twang that speaks humor and sorrow at the same time. One can easily listen to speech that climbs and falls like the gentle red dirt hills of Alabama. If you watch movies and television, you might think all of us below the Mason-Dixon Line talk alike, but we don't. Not at all.

A woman from Georgia once told me she had been to Fort Smith, Arkansas.

"I couldn't believe that drawl they have out there," she said. "Is that real?"

When I heard her speak, I heard peach trees and antebellum cotillions. Desire and romance rushed through me although she was at least two decades older.

Social scientists say that men, more than women, are attracted by visual appearance. Not me, at least not foremost. It is sound that captures my heart like when Little Debbie asked why the windshield wipers were on—the beginning and the end of one of the great romances of my imagination.

During the first week of school during my freshman year at a west coast university, I had to read a selection from a text out loud in class. The reading was humorous but not guffaw, laugh-out loud funny. By the time I finished, though, my classmates roared. These Californians were an easy audience, I thought. Then the professor cleared his throat.

"We shouldn't laugh at people who speak with an accent that is different from our own," he said. "We all speak with an accent."

The other students were laughing at me, not with me, not at the selection I had just read. They had laughed at the regional markers of my voice, ones that sounded the same to them regardless of whether my speech had come from Tahlequah, Oklahoma or Itta Bena, Mississippi.

Despite the apparent truth of my teacher's observation, I heard over and over again during my years in the far West: "We don't have an accent out here."

More often than not, it took the form of a boast, and it still impresses me as rather sad. What kind of a brag is it for a voice not to have an accent? It's like chicken fried steak made without black pepper, like a kitchen without aromas, an opera without arias, coffee without a kick. When I step off an airplane returning from someplace else, it is the native sound I hear that makes my heart dance.

Maybe, though, my classmates who told me "we don't have an accent out here" were more prescient and right than my professor who gracefully tried to salve my hurt feelings.

The voices on cable television all sound alike now, just as a box store in Raleigh is identical to a box store in Sioux Falls, and a frozen mass-produced pie tastes the same in Fort Worth as it does in Seattle. When I hear a newscaster on the radio, I wonder where she is from, what life lies behind her. I can't tell by listening. The voices that speak to us impersonally come to us from nowhere with no past.

Maybe that is what sparks the desire and makes our hearts dance: Our accents reminds us of a place called home and echo our unrehearsed past.

Life Without GPS
July 2008

Two years ago, my wife, Jackie, and I took our fifteen-year-old nephew, Nick, to Western Oklahoma to visit the places Nick's grandparents, great-grandparents, and great-great grandparents lived and settled.

In the 1960's and 1970's, United Methodist ministers in Oklahoma moved on average every three or four years. By the age of fifteen, I had lived in seven different parsonages in six different towns and had never slept on a mattress owned by my parents. Until my father was promoted into supervisory and administrative positions, every move meant a new church and a new place to play hide and seek.

Churches on weekdays are the best places to play hide and seek. Musty classrooms, dark sacristies, hidden halls, and funky places to crawl—places adults never visit. Each church provided new places to hide, to seek, to discover, and to find. A Global Positioning System (GPS) would have destroyed the fun.

GPS monitors your location by U.S. Department of Defense satellite and provides computerized directions from one place to another. It's a great invention for emergency vehicles, big city driving, and those perpetually lost, but I doubt I'll ever own one by my own election. If you always know where you're going, that's the only place you'll find.

In Western Oklahoma, the sky spreads one hundred and eighty degrees from one horizon to another, interrupted only by a few scraggly trees and windbreaks. Before the white people came, the Plains Indians hunted buffalo on this prairie land. Early maps identify this stretch of Oklahoma and Kansas as "The Great

American Desert." Now the red earth breaks open to grow golden grains and sprouts short gray-green grass over which domesticated Angus and Hereford graze.

Except.

The land surprises. After miles and miles of flatland, mesas arise glittering in the sun. A turn off the main road and you may breathe the salt scents of an ancient sea and feel the sand beneath your feet. Canyons cut into the earth unnoticed and flora and fauna change from high plains with scrub trees and cactus to forest and water.

With so much sky and flatland and wind, we grow numb and forget the land's surprise and that the land, like the churches of my childhood, provides the best places to seek, discover, and find. When our purpose is simply to get from one place to another, wonder hides so well it disappears. We lose the gift of childhood when we stop playing hide and seek.

Jackie, Nick, and I checked into a cabin at a state park located in one of these Western Oklahoma canyons. In the 1800's, a band of Southern Cheyenne led by Chief Roman Nose would winter here, protected as it is from the Great Plains winds by canyon walls and forest.

I wanted to show Nick so much out on the Oklahoma flatlands. The big white house in Okeene where his great-grandmother reigned, the remains of her husband's first hardware store, the family farm staked in a land rush, the little town—Custer City—Nick's great-great grandfather helped settle, the courthouse in Arapaho where my Grandpa Darrah judged, and the obscure cemeteries where our mutual predecessors lie buried. These, the constant places of my gypsy childhood. Our time was short.

We traveled to family monuments by day and returned to the Roman Nose cabin at twilight, hot and expended. One of those evenings, we decided to swim in the park's WPA-era swimming pool. We changed into our swimsuits and walked to the canyon meadow to cool off in the swimming pool's water, only to find the facility closed that day.

"Let's look around," Jackie suggested as she wandered away, not caring whether her husband and nephew followed. When she reached the meadow's edge, she called, "There's a stream here. We can play in it."

Can't hurt to look, I thought, knowing, of course, the creeks and rivers of the Plains are always unfriendly, slow-moving, brackish, and muddy.

Not this stream. Not at all. Cool, clear water bubbled and raced over rocks and tree roots along a shallow bed against the canyon wall.

Nick, Jackie, and I stepped into the water so cold it drew goose bumps in June. As we played in the stream and hiked upstream towards a thicket of trees, a man appeared at the woods' edge. He wore khaki sans-a-belt slacks, a plaid sports shirt, gold-rimmed glasses, and a narrow-brimmed houndstooth fedora. A hefty man of perhaps seventy-five or eighty summers.

Probably here to hassle us about playing in the stream, I thought.

Who would have complained, though? We had seen no one since we had left our cabin for the swimming pool. The earth was still and silent except for the slight sound of rumbling ahead.

"Good evening," the man said. "It's a beautiful evening, isn't it?"

"Ooh, this water's just too cold," Jackie said as she got out of the stream, but Nick and I kept playing and hiking in the creek's tiny rapids.

"I come here often and walk a bit," the man said. "It never quite looks the same, but it's always beautiful."

"The pool was closed," Jackie said, "so we decided to cool off here."

"Don't blame you at all," the old man said. "If I got around better, I might join you. Can't now. Got a little stiffness but that's one of the reasons I walk. Doctor says I might have to start using a cane. I'm going to disappoint him."

By now, my feet were numb and I, too, stepped onto the bank. He asked where we were from and what brought us here. Jackie explained.

I continued, "My grandfather used to have the hardware store in Okeene. Beckloff's Hardware and Farm Implements."

The man nodded. "Your Uncle Shorty used to barber my hair when I had more hair to barber."

The old man said his name was Ted Jasper. He lived in nearby Watonga and had worked in real estate most of his life.

"You ever seen the springs that feed this creek?" he asked.

Is there anywhere people can go anymore where they can be left alone? I wondered. We just want to play in the water. We just want to cool off. The springs can't be much of anything. This is Western Oklahoma. Maybe we'll see it later. Maybe not. Thank you anyway.

"You really need to see the springs. It's where Roman Nose used to camp," he said. "Let me show you." He started walking back into the woods and we followed, somehow knowing we had to.

The June twilight sun fell in beams and prisms through the hickory and oak canopy. Slabs of sandstone cluttered the forest floor and wild squirrels rattled the limbs of the redbud trees. The rumbling grew louder as we continued into the woods.

Typical Oklahoma state government, I thought. Somebody's drilling an oil well within feet of a state park. Maybe in the state park.

"My wife died two years ago," the man said.

"I'm sorry," Jackie said.

"Just about every night since, I've come here and walked," the man said.

As Jackie and the old man continued up the nearby path, I stepped back into the stream and joined Nick on the hike into the woods. The water grew colder and deeper the further we walked. The rumbling grew louder and the current, stronger.

The water gushed over bigger rocks and the incline steepened. Each step seemed less secure. I looked to the path. Jackie and the old man were gone. I got out of the water to find them, to follow them.

I walked fast through the yellow light and over the spindly feet of the elm and walnut trees. The rocky path curved and climbed. The rumbling grew louder and louder and louder. I turned past a clump of trees and found myself in a prairie rainforest where the earth smelled of potter's clay and the air touched the skin like ancient mist.

Jackie and Ted Jasper stood by a pool of water next to an opening in the rusty gray canyon wall where clear water—gallons, gallons, and gallons—poured out, roaring, roaring, and rumbling.

"This," the old man called out, "is the Spring of Everlasting Waters."

The Spring of Everlasting Waters?

The Spring of Ever Lasting Waters.

The Spring of Ever Flowing Waters.

We stood at the place where Chief Roman Nose led his people, to the springs where the clear water ever flows, to the source where life always begins and maintains. We paused here, then reached down and touched the cold, stirring pool.

Later, Ted Jasper led us further into the woods and showed us three other beautiful, but smaller, springs. When we separated that night, he gave us his card and told us to call him if we were ever back in the area, but

I'm not sure he really exists anywhere except in that wooded canyon on certain summer nights.

So keep your GPS. It may tell you where you are and how to get where you want to go. It'll never, though, show you where ancient souls wander dressed as small town Kiwanians or the springs of everlasting water.

Boxes and Cans
December 1997

My brother collects cans. I collect boxes. Empty, worthless cans, and empty, worthless boxes. My wife has almost broken me of that habit. Maybe my brother's wife has almost broken him of his, too.

Cans are great to put little things in. Like nails and bolts and screws. Little things that hold bigger things together, to make other things work. Boxes come in all sizes, but I like the ones that are big and sturdy, that can comfortably pack books. Books that tell stories and teach history and lessons.

It has become somewhat in vogue to write about the metaphysics of fishing—fly-fishing in particular. I've never fly-fished but I have a hard time thinking of fishing as a metaphor for life, or how a person becomes one with his rig, or with the fish, or with nature. It reminds me of the advice a yuppie fisherman once gave me: Wear surgical gloves when you fish; it'll keep your hands from smelling so bad.

I know what my grandfather would say about that. Probably the same thing he used to say about fishing with trotlines.

"That's not fishing," he would say derisively without much other explanation. And, he wasn't usually one to be derisive or to not say much more.

Trotlines are fishing rigs that you can bait, drop into a lake, leave, and pull out hours later with all the fish that voluntarily ate the bait without any effort on your part other than you dropping the rig into the water. Trotline fishing brings in the largest number of fish with the least effort. I like to think that part of Grandpa's aversion to trotline fishing was that it was cruel and wasteful because we never kept all the fish we caught anyway. I think Grandpa's real aversion to it, though, was the lack of skill and craft it demonstrated.

My brother and I used to go fishing with my grandfather. The last time I went with him I was eight years old; my brother three years older. Sometimes my grandmother would go with us. Sometimes, others. The times I remember best, though, are when it was just the three of us: My brother, my grandfather, and me.

We would leave in late afternoon. Grandma would have packed up butter sandwiches and a thermos of hot, strong coffee. We would load up the car, go to the lake, get in Grandpa's boat, and fish until about dusk when we tied up under a bridge to fish until late at night. In truth, I wasn't much of a fisherman. Grandma later regaled in telling that I liked to go fishing just so that I could take a leak in the can that Grandpa kept in the boat so we wouldn't have to go to shore or risk falling into the lake when nature called.

Even though I wasn't much of a fisherman—I was too young—I enjoyed those evenings. We'd sit in the boat with the lines in the water. Grandpa would have a cup of coffee by his side. An errant minnow would accidentally flip into his cup and Grandpa would fish it out.

"Grandpa, aren't you going to throw out that coffee?" He'd shake his head and reply: "It makes it taste better."

Grandpa would tell stories, talk about history and politics, and teach us lessons like no man is better or worse than you because of the color of his skin, or by what they have or don't have. Civil Liberties 101 taught in a boat on Lake Texhoma by an old man to two young boys.

That was the way it was with Grandpa. He treated us like two little men. I don't remember him ever reprimanding us but I don't remember us being on anything but our good behavior either. Perhaps because he treated us like two little men, we acted like two little men. When we were with Grandpa on the lake, everything seemed OK. He loved us, and we knew he did.

I wish I had a recording of his stories, his talks, his lessons. I can still hear his voice, but I can't hear his words, not exactly. I hope I learned what he taught. I hope my life reflects that, but it would be nice to hear the stories or to read their exact words.

Grandpa was also a good fisherman. I didn't appreciate that skill, but I think my brother did. Grandpa's fishing rigs were tied nice and tidy so they wouldn't come apart. He knew what weights to use, what size hooks were best, and the baits that attracted which fish. He knew how to tie all these little things together to make them work. My brother says that in the years since we fished with Grandpa, he has learned, and forgotten, how others have taught him to tie fishing rigs together, but he remembers every knot Grandpa showed him.

I could finish this piece by saying that fishing with Grandpa was some kind of metaphysical experience or perhaps I just liked taking a leak in a coffee can. I won't. Grandpa wouldn't approve. This I know: My brother likes to build things to make them work. I like stories, history, and lessons.

My brother collects cans. I collect boxes.

Into the Secret Present
July 2000

Uncle George drank himself to death, but I've never heard anyone say that. He did, though. At her high school reunion that year, my mother wouldn't even admit he had died. "He's taking a long vacation," my mother would answer inquiring classmates.

One from which he'll never return.

My family keeps secrets.

Family lore held I resemble George more than anyone else among his relatives. I no longer drink, but I wonder whether the demons that keep me awake at night are the same demons George saw in the darkness or when he looked in the mirror. And, if so, do they from generation to generation pass?

My grandmother—George's mother—never talked much about her father, my great-grandfather. He was an Irish tenor and a drunk. He often just disappeared for days, weeks, years. He would then show up and be gone as quickly as he came. He died in 1946. That was about all I knew. Maybe if I could learn my great-grandfather's story, I would understand George better, understand me better.

In search of my great-grandfather's story, my wife, Jackie, and I traveled in 1995 to Kidder, Missouri, the pastoral hamlet where my grandmother grew up. The local historian determined a woman named Ida Look may have known my grandmother. When I called Miss Look, she said: "I was expecting your call. Please come visit."

Ida Look and her sister, Persis Courter, lived in a tidy yellow duplex. Ida had soft-looking skin and a wise and kind smile. Persis was a large woman with an impish and impulsive grin. Ida wore a faded yellow housedress; Persis's arm was bandaged. They apologized again and again that their house wasn't cleaner; they both had been sick. Ida had been born in 1910; Persis, in 1907.

"We are about the only ones who would know anything about your family," Ida said from her faux velvet green recliner.

Persis interrupted. "There might be one lady who would know more, but her mind is too far gone. Would you please go into the kitchen? It's a little hard for me to get around."

I left Jackie in the living room with the two sisters. I went into the kitchen and looked and waited for my next instruction. A hand-crocheted washcloth sat on the kitchen table.

"Take that dishcloth," Persis said from the living room. "I want to give it to you before I forget."

"That's kind, but you don't need to..." I said.

"We want to thank you for coming."

How long had they been waiting for someone from their childhood past to visit? I picked up the dishcloth woven of time and patience and returned to the living room, carrying the gift.

Ida remembered my grandmother. "She had dark hair and dark eyes. She was very dark. She was in everything. Every play or production at the Kidder Institute. We worked together as telephone operators right after high school. There was a bad accident. She was beside herself. The man she would marry..."

"My grandfather," I said.

"The truck he was in was hit up the side by the Hannibal-St. Joe train, there at the crossing. Oh, she was beside herself. She was..."

"Overdramatic?" I asked.

"Not overdramatic," Ida said. "I would say she overreacted."

"I haven't been able to figure out where Grandma's family lived."

"The Morgan place is the second house past the railroad track," Ida said.

"We still refer to the places by who lived in them back then," Persis added, "even though most of those families no longer live there."

"The Morgan place isn't there anymore," Ida continued. "The volunteer fire department needed practice putting out a fire. That old house had fallen down and was dilapidated, so they set it aflame and put it out."

Then I asked the question I had traveled over three hundred miles to ask: "Did you know my great-grandfather?"

"Oh, no," Ida said. "We didn't move here until 1916."

"Yes," said Persis. "He was already dead by then."

Jackie started to speak, started to tell Ida Look and Persis Courter that my absentee great-grandfather didn't die until 1946.

I touched Jackie's arm and shook my head.

Jackie understood. She didn't speak.

My family keeps secrets.

A Name Is a Name For All That
May 2011

I'm still waiting for someone to name a child after me. Mark Stephen, if it's a boy. Marketa Stephanie, if it's a girl. I've had no takers. Neither set of names make anyone's top one hundred list. Still, if I were a rich childless oilman, I bet someone would be happy to call their little tyke T. Boone or T. Boonetta.

In the meantime, I just wait.

The liberal arts college at my alma mater recently changed its name to honor some donors who made a huge financial contribution to my university. The gift was certainly generous, and the university rightly recognized the donors. Still, like most alums, I know nothing about these benefactors or whether they merit having a place of learning named after them. These namesake donors may think that the first shots of the Revolutionary War were fired in New Hampshire or that Shakespeare is a type of martini. Maybe the folks who gave this large gift illegally smuggle guns into the heart of Africa. Maybe they traffic in orphan slave trade. I simply don't know.

Maybe someone would name a liberal arts college after me if I gave the school a cash gift of nine figures.

Today, names of public spaces are sold, and the location of a public event becomes an advertisement. In Tulsa, Texas League baseball is played on Oneok Field. The QuikTrip Center hosts a midget car race. Lady Gaga creates a spectacle at the BOK Center. Just like my liberal arts college, the city and the county got a bunch of money for naming these public places after these companies. That's probably a good thing. Does it really matter whether these nonhuman corporations merit having facilities named after them if our community gets easy money in return?

The original science building at the University of Oklahoma was named after Doctor Edwin C. DeBarr, one of the university's four founding professors. In 1988, OU changed the structure's designation from DeBarr Hall to the Chemistry Building, a pedestrian sounding title for sure, but one that doesn't honor an active Klansman as Professor DeBarr apparently was. He wasn't alone in Oklahoma. In 1925, every candidate for Speaker of the House was a Klansmen, and the KKK actively and successfully recruited in Baptist, Methodist, and other white Protestant churches.

If Doctor DeBarr had given a fortune to OU, would the university have changed the name of his building? Would he not have purchased the naming rights?

In recent years, activists have sought to have Murray Hall at Oklahoma State University retitled. The moniker of the recently remodeled building on the Stillwater campus recognizes William "Alfalfa Bill" Murray, one of Oklahoma early governors and a stridently unpleasant racist and anti-Semite. While Murray's efforts at statehood helped insure the enactment of Jim Crow laws, Murray also wrote most of our state's constitution, a landmark charter that guaranteed participatory government and which enshrined protections for workers, farmers, and the poor.

Should Murray Hall remain Murray Hall?

This naming business gets complicated.

I recently drove past Tulsa County Stadium at 15th and Yale. It used to be called Driller Stadium because our city's professional baseball team played there. When the facility opened in 1981, it was called Sutton Stadium since a large gift by Tulsa oilman Bob Sutton financed its construction. After Sutton's federal court convictions for obstruction of justice and conspiracy to commit the same, his name was removed from the ballpark. That never seemed right to me. Sutton's generosity still made the building of the ballpark possible. Like BOK, Oneok, and QuikTrip, Sutton had purchased the naming rights, hadn't he?

An old man called recently. He told me he had named his son after my grandfather, a prohibition-era county judge in western Oklahoma. The caller said he always got his liquor from my judge grandfather because the town bootlegger sold it to Grandpa at half-price as a professional courtesy.

Public venues now advertise imperfect corporations with no compunction. When we honor someone by bestowing his or her name on another person or place, we must do so with the knowledge that the person honored—because of his or her humanity—is inherently imperfect.

So, I wait for little Mark Stephen or little Marketa Stephanie.

Maybe it's like what my brother says about being cool. If you have to tell someone you're cool, you aren't.

Maybe if you have to ask someone to name a kid after you, you really don't deserve it.

Maybe I should think about buying naming rights.

My Family Eats Pizza
On Christmas Eve

December 2006

My family eats pizza on Christmas Eve.

The tradition began as an accommodation. Actually, a double accommodation.

My father is a United Methodist minister. He spent his adult life preaching the Good News, telling the most troubled they are important in God's sight, holding the hands of those who have lost loved ones, assuring the hopeless that hope prevails, and befriending those without friends.

Christmas was his busy season.

Our tradition of eating pizza on Christmas Eve began because of two events. First, the red-brick hobby store a block from the church where my father pastored had been torn down and a shining new Pizza Hut had replaced it. And second, about same time, a new Christmas Eve service began at our church so families could enjoy their time together and also stop for a moment of reflection without too much inconvenience.

The Christmas Eve service was my father's idea. It began at least at his instigation. Dad called it "Come and Go" Communion. From seven to nine o'clock on Christmas Eve, parishioners—and anyone else for that matter—could come into the sanctuary for a time of silence and a sharing of the Eucharist.

"Come and Go" Communion accommodated everyone's schedule on Christmas Eve, except for the pastor and his family. With Dad leaving early to open the church and prepare for the service and staying unpredictably late, ordering pizza for supper from the new Pizza Hut when Dad returned accommodated his family's schedule. That took care of supper, but not my parents' two youngest children who were eager to get on with celebrating Christmas on Christmas Eve.

So my father took my sister and me with him to church on Christmas Eve.

On this most special night of the year, we got to be ushers, just like those stalwart men in handsome suits on Sunday morning, but we didn't get to take up collection.

The church was decades old with creaky floors and beautiful stained glass windows. It was a space of reverence, of old heavy woods and funny antique smells. On Christmas Eve, the church seemed darker than any other night of the year. On this night, every soul that had sought mercy in that sanctuary seemed to hum quietly in its very walls. On this night, every prayer ever offered there lingered faintly, a constant testimony to faith.

What my sister and I liked best about the service— besides getting to usher—was that there was no sermon. While my father was putting on his black robe, Linda and I would run upstairs to the Alois Classroom and check the light on the big stained-glass window so that those entering the church, or simply passing by, could see the image of Jesus shining through the night.

Back downstairs in the sanctuary, the communion elements—grape juice and wafers—had been placed in shiny gold trays and put beneath white linen on the communion table. Gold candelabra stood on each side, holding a thousand candles it seemed. Every electric light in the sanctuary was out except for a few directly above the chancel, leaving the place shadowy black. At a few minutes before seven, Linda and I lit the candles and my father began the service.

Ye that do truly and earnestly repent of your sins, and are in love and charity with your neighbors, and intend to lead a new life, draw near with faith and take this holy sacrament to your comfort...

Linda and I would move quietly to the side and then to the back of the sanctuary. Sometimes no one else would be present, just the three of us for the ritual and no more.

Hear what comfortable words the Scriptures say. Come to me, all who labor and are heavy laden, and I will give you rest.

From the back of the sanctuary, we could see Dad standing by the white linen-covered table, reciting the liturgy as if he had written it himself; the light from the candles shining like hope in a world of darkness.

And we most humbly beseech thee, of thy goodness, O Lord, to support and strengthen all those who, in this transitory life, are in trouble, sorrow, need, sickness, or any other adversity.

It seemed strange that on Christmas Eve, the night of Christ's birth, we remembered Christ's death.

Who in the same night that he was betrayed, took bread: and when he had given thanks, he broke it, and gave to his disciples, saying... Likewise, after supper, he took the cup...

When the liturgy was over and all that remained was serving the bread and the cup to those who came and went, Linda and I went and waited in the narthex. We welcomed those who came, opening the doors for them, telling them "Merry Christmas," and aggravating each other. As much as anything, our presence there as Christmas Eve ushers let my mother and older brother be at peace at home without a couple of hyperactive Christmas-crazed kids driving them nuts.

Therefore with angels and archangels, and with all the company of heaven, we laud and magnify thy glorious name, evermore praising thee, and saying:

Holy, holy, holy, Lord God of hosts: Heaven and earth are full of thy glory! Glory be to thee, O Lord most High! Amen.

My family will be eating pizza this Christmas Eve. It won't be from that Pizza Hut. It's been torn down and replaced with a prototype McDonald's. My father won't be eating pizza at all. He is now seventy-nine years old. The last four he has spent as a nursing home resident. All his food is pureed because he can no longer chew, one of the debilitations of Parkinson's disease.

I would tell you that I would happily kick the worthless ass of any radio show host who makes fun of those destroyed by this disease, but as I type, I can hear my father reprimanding my language and its violence. Actually, Dad no longer speaks. At least, not often or more than a few words. Parkinson's not only steals the ability to move; it often makes the mind unable to work. My father is almost completely paralyzed now, unable to do anything for himself, unable to verbalize thought or memory.

His room at the nursing home is like most others at nursing homes. There is a string to pull to call a nurse. Fluorescent lights line the walls near the ceiling to provide indirect lighting so that the aides can have enough light to do their work without waking the patients. Over my father's bed, there is a picture of Jesus looking over Dad and all those who enter and pass by.

On Christmas Eve night, I will go to visit my father. The light will be off in his room. I will tell him I love him and as I leave, I'll turn on that indirect light so that it may shine like hope in the darkness.

Becoming Barney Fife
(A Tale of Woeful Governance)
July 2006

To some, choosing a manager for the neighborhood swimming pool had no more significance than a cicada's buzz on an August night in the Ozarks. To the board of directors making the decision, though, a mistake risked causing a shift of the earth's tectonic plates.

I was thirty when I bought my first house, a California home with a flat roof and narrow flagstone. In the 1950's, our subdivision was space age cool. Every house had boomerang Formica and picture windows. Another neat-o feature was the neighborhood swimming pool, operated by volunteers and paid for by voluntary dues.

At thirty-one, I became the president of the nonprofit that ran the neighborhood pool. Being president was of no reward: Irate parents, surprise health department inspections, no-show volunteers, and never enough money to pay all the bills.

The big top moment of my term occurred when a lifeguard lost her swimsuit top as she attempted to pull a panicked child out of the water. I missed it, of course, and the board of directors immediately instituted The One-Piece Swimsuit Rule for All Lifeguards for All Eternity. (The motion carried like an avalanche and the president—me—had no vote except in the event of a tie. So instead, I imagined drowning myself before our lifeguards bought the full-body replacements.)

I had never wanted to grow up. Oh sure, I had wanted to be able to drive a Maserati and to buy Wild Turkey liqueur, but I had never wanted to mow the yard on weekends, pay bills, or become rigid and grouchy like most adults.

At thirty-one, I was into resume building and public service, but owning my own home and becoming president of the neighborhood pool made me feel like an adult. Being a grown-up overwhelmed me like death, particularly at parties with people my own age. I hated standing around, sipping imported beer, talking about home improvements, lawn maintenance, and potty training.

Now the board of directors of the neighborhood pool had to make a decision. Two high school girls had been chosen as finalists for the life-guarding positions before I became president, but one of the teenagers had to be designated "Pool Manager" because of health department regulations.

The first candidate, the almost seventeen-year-old Christine, had the body of Venus de Milo and about the same brainpower. Christine carried herself with a certain brittleness, the result most likely of too much time in Southern Baptist Sunday School.

Julie, the other pool manager candidate, was everybody's buddy, a future heartbreaker or home wrecker of a country song. Julie was sixteen, a round-faced blonde with lazy blue eyes, and had breasts that threw shadows on her feet.

Christine and Julie both had passed the Red Cross Lifesaving course with no problem. Both had good references. Both were equally qualified to be "Pool Manager."

Except Christine hated Julie and Julie hated Christine. And, half the pool board hated Christine while the other half hated Julie. I never knew why and no one would tell me. Kind of like the Balkan wars. Regardless, one of the young women had to be selected "Pool Manager."

The brilliance and absurdity of democracy is compromise, so that is what we did. Both girls would lifeguard, work the same number of hours and weekends, and be paid the same wage. Both could have one after-hours pool party for their friends, but the stiff and brittle Christine would be designated "Pool Manager" because she was a couple months older than the supple and easy-going Julie.

It was a tenuous solution. Christine spent the summer trying to sabotage Julie and Julie spent the summer trying to sabotage Christine. I never knew who or what to believe.

One evening, I arrived at the pool for a board of directors meeting. Something seemed wrong. The place was too tidy, too peaceful, too serene.

Christine, our pool manager, made an announcement just as the board meeting began. "Julie is having a pool party tonight" she said, "and it is going to be really wild. She's going to have like a thousand people here. She's going to serve beer, and she's even hired a bouncer. She took the hanging potted plants down so they won't get, you know, ruined. I just thought the board ought to know."

Christine sashayed away. The board members looked at each other in silence, knowing the party couldn't be. The silence burst into uproar. Christine's fans cranked up the sound the loudest:

"Julie's party has to be stopped."

"A wild party, my God! No way! No way, by God!"

"Julie's irresponsible behavior risks everything."

No one spoke in opposition. No one asked if Christine's claims were true. The hanging plants were down—a clear sign of swimming pool debauchery. Without a vote, the decision had been made: No party for Julie.

Then, one of her fans spoke in a quiet, squeaky voice: "Christine is supposed to have her party here in two weeks. We have to cancel Christine's party, too, if we don't let Julie have hers."

"Christine won't have a party with beer and bouncers," one of Christine's stalwarts snapped.

"Besides," said another, "we have to keep Christine content. She is going to have to do all the life-guarding the two weeks Julie is off for her breast reduction surgery."

"What!" the board's matriarch exclaimed. "Hell, she hasn't even had 'em long enough to know if she likes 'em!"

I was glad someone else said that.

Then Barbara, our most sensible board member, spoke up: "That's just a ridiculous rumor Christine started so we would pander to her every little whim. Julie is scheduled to work the entire summer. Another girl is life-guarding this party. Everything that can be broken has been put away. She has a bouncer to keep things from getting too crazy, for God's sake! She's trying to be responsible. What would it say about us if we told her she couldn't have the party we had promised her less than two hours before it was supposed to begin?"

The board reached another brilliant and absurd compromise. The president—me—would have a firm talk with Julie beforehand about responsibility and under-aged drinking, but Julie would have her party.

She showed up with some friends a few minutes after the board meeting adjourned. I took her to the side and put on my best Sheriff Andy Taylor facade. If I had to be an authoritarian, I wanted to do it like Andy Griffith did in Mayberry, not as Joe Friday did on the streets of LA.

"Julie, the board has gotten some reports that your party tonight is going to be—well, pretty exciting. Now, we all want you to have a good time. We really do, but we want everyone safe. We're expecting you to keep the noise down and there will be no under-age drinking. Period. OK?"

Julie smiled, bobbed her head from side to side, and said, "'K!"

And there it was.

I'd become an adult.

About ten-thirty that night, I started getting ready for bed. I went into the bathroom and I heard teen party noise. The neighborhood swimming pool was about five miles away from my home as the crow flies (since they fly mainly in circles) but only about a block away if I could walk straight from my front door to the pool which I couldn't. I shrugged and thought the party noise would pass. I started brushing my teeth. The air-conditioning compressor outside the bathroom window kicked on. I could still hear the noise. The uproar wasn't fading. I sighed. The Board President was going to have to enforce the rules at Julie's party. I had to be an adult. I got dressed.

The night was damp and hot. As I got closer to the pool, I got even more steamed. The neighbors are going to complain, I thought. I'll get telephone calls for the rest of the summer and probably into the winter. Maybe for the rest of my life. If the police aren't at the pool yet, they soon will be. The board members and volunteers who wanted to cancel Julie's party will quit. I'll have to deal with upset parents. It'll end up being me alone with one of those stupid butterfly nets scooping dead leaves out of the pool while fifty screaming kids try to drown each other because no one else was idiot enough to allow themselves to get elected president of the board and everybody else has quit!

As I got closer to the pool, Sheriff Andy Taylor became Charles Bronson with a death wish.

I walked through the gate of the privacy fence that led to the neighborhood pool and saw about forty teenagers—in the water, at its edge, on top of picnic tables, and some groping each other in the shadows beneath the trees on the far side. A lawn chair sat at the bottom of the pool and a thrown living human being hit the surface as I walked in. Electronic bubble-gum music blasted from a pulsating oversized boom box.

I didn't see Julie anywhere.

I slithered around partying teenagers to the table where refreshments were served and looked into an ice chest. It was half full of beer. A kid stood there with a can of Budweiser in his hand. I stood silently and surveyed the party. No discussion of home improvements, lawn maintenance, or potty training here.

"Great party, isn't it?" the kid with the beer in his hand said.

I nodded.

"Are you a friend of Julie's?" he asked.

"Yeah," I said, "but I'm also the president of the organization that runs this place."

The kid paused for a teenaged second. "It's really great of you guys to let Julie have a party. It's a great party. There's plenty of beer here if you want one.

I looked at the half-full ice chest. "Thanks," I said, "but we can't have any under-age drinking at the pool. You know how that goes. How old are you?"

"Just turned eighteen," the kid said without a pause.

Fifteen, I thought. "Do you see Julie around here?"

"No, but she's somewhere. Do you want me to go find her?"

"No. I'll just wait until she comes around." I liked the kid, even though he lied about his age. I would have coughed up eighteen, too. I stood and watched the party in awe.

A few minutes later, Julie climbed out of a mass of bodies in the swimming pool and walked over. The One-Piece Bathing Suit Rule hadn't been put into effect for private parties and Julie's over-packed bikini was white, tight, wet, and dripping.

"Julie," I stammered and muttered. "Y'all are going to have to cool it a bit. I don't want the neighbors calling the police on you and you'd feel rotten if somebody got hurt. Just tone it down some and watch the drinking, OK?"

Julie smiled, bobbed her head from side to side, and said, "'K!"

"Thanks. Just keep it cool."

In the presence of a sixteen year-old with a bosom that threw shadows on her feet, I had morphed from Charles Bronson to Barney Fife without even stopping at Joe Friday or Andy Griffith.

I never wanted to be an adult anyway.

As I walked through that gate to leave, the music softened and the party sounds diminished to peaceful all the way home. The police didn't show up. Nobody was hurt. No neighbors complained. None of the pool volunteers quit or said, "I told you so." Most of that came when Christine had her party two weeks later, but that's another story.

As I got into bed that night, the air-conditioning compressor kicked on and over its decrepit wheeze, I heard once more the unending roar of teenaged joy from the neighborhood swimming pool.

God, it was a great party.

Bob Wills and the Dancing Cowgirl
December 1997

I embarrass my wife. When you go to a baseball game anymore, you aren't invited to join in the singing of the national anthem. Someone else sings "The Star Spangled Banner" for you. I don't know when this started, but I don't like it. There's nothing wrong with my voice (and maybe not yours either). So, when Jackie and I go to the ball game and we are asked to rise for the singing of the national anthem, I don't just stand there and listen. I bellow it out. Like I said, I embarrass my wife.

If I could sing so you would enjoy it, I would. If I could play an instrument well enough to give you pleasure, I would play for you. As it is, allow me just to tell you some of my favorite stories—some legends actually—about music and musicians.

~~~

Waylon Jennings wrote a song that claims in Texas, Bob Wills is still the king. The verse may be right, but if it weren't for Oklahoma, Bob Wills would never have been made king in the first place. You see, his biggest career boost came from being kicked out of the Lone Star State.

As a young man, Bob worked as a barber in Turkey, Texas, a small panhandle town where his family settled when he was a boy. There, he learned to play the fiddle and the songs of the old West. After cutting one or two many heads of hair, Wills moved to Fort Worth where he worked by day for Burrus Mills, a grain milling company. At night and over the noon hour, he fiddled for a band called The Light Crust Doughboys, which advertised Burrus Mills' flour.

The milling company was managed by W. Lee "Pass the Biscuits, Pappy" O'Daniel who attached himself to the band and later became governor of Texas, due largely to the fame he acquired by being associated with The Light Crust Doughboys. On nights the band didn't play, Wills and the other Doughboys would travel to Dallas, go to the juke joints, and listen to the black musicians playing there. Bob Wills, together with the inspiration of Milton Brown, fused these sounds with the folk tunes of west Texas, the mariachi sounds of Mexico, and created what is now known as "Western Swing," even though he couldn't read a note of music.

By the early 1930's, The Light Crust Doughboys were tremendously popular, especially because of the radio shows that touted Burrus Mills flour. Problems arose between Wills and "Pass the Biscuits, Pappy," the origins of which are not precisely known. Some say it was because the band members had to work in the mill during the day as well as play music at night. Some say it was because Wills liked his liquor and women too much. Others say it was because O'Daniel's religious beliefs prohibited the Doughboys from playing dances.

Regardless, Bob Wills formed a band called The Playboys, quit the mill, and made a pass at playing a live show at a competing radio station. W. Lee "Pass the Biscuits, Pappy" O'Daniel called the station and threatened to pull the Burrus Mills advertising if The Playboys played on the air. Fort Worth turned off the lights on the band before they even came on.

Bob and his comrades took their music to Waco where they began playing on another radio station. O'Daniel heard about it and sued Wills and several others for referring to themselves as "former members of The Light Crust Doughboys." Bob and the boys began to understand they were no longer welcome at home.

They moved to Oklahoma City and started a show on WKY. O'Daniel called the station and promised the manager he would arrange for WKY to carry The Light Crust Doughboys' broadcasts if only he'd get rid of the Texas Playboys. It never happened (remember W. Lee would become a Texas governor), but once again, Bob and his band lost their playing gig.

The musical refugees moved to Tulsa and began to play on KVOO, the 25,000 watt Voice of Oklahoma whose powerful broadcasts reached across the country. "Pass the Biscuits, Pappy" telephoned and told the station owner the Burrus Mills advertising would be lost if the Playboys stayed on the air. The owner told O'Daniel that he owned the station in fee simple and no Texas SOB was going to tell him what he could or could not do.

Bob Wills and the Texas Playboys went on to broadcast a live noon show on KVOO every weekday and played Cain's Ballroom almost every weekend in the 1930's and early 1940's, making Tulsa the capital of Western Swing. During those discouraging days of the Great Depression, the band played music that made people all across the country laugh and dance and remember life means hope.

So tell me: Would Bob Wills have been king if the future governor of Texas hadn't tried to silence the music?

~~~

The animosity between Bob Wills and "Pass the Biscuits, Pappy" never reconciled. Although The Light Crust Doughboys went on to record some classic songs of their own, they were never invited to and never played in Tulsa—a courtesy to Bob and his band. That is, until a few years ago when a soulless mega-bookstore decided to feature The Light Crust Doughboys at its grand opening. I suppose having the band was some middle manager's mistaken idea of ingratiating the store with the community.

As a matter of loyalty, I thought I shouldn't go. When, though, would I ever have the chance to hear The Light Crust Doughboys again? I had to go. Sixty years is too long to hold a grudge anyway. To this day, though, I refrain from buying at that store and don't intend to change my habits either.

The Light Crust Doughboys attracted a good crowd that afternoon. As I stood waiting for the music to begin, I noticed next to me an old bent-back man and his little gray-haired wife. The man told me he had never heard The Light Crust Doughboys play in person. Then he whispered, "In the 1930's, I wore cardboard in my shoes, but every Saturday night I had four bits to get the wife and me into Cain's Ballroom to hear Bob Wills and the Texas Playboys."

~~~

"Make the audience happy they're alive," Bob Wills would tell the band. "Make 'em forget their troubles. Smile at the folks in the audience. Smile at the people on the dance floor. They're payin' us to get away from their troubles."

At one of those Saturday night dances at Cain's, the Texas Playboys, as usual, followed Bob's direction and smiled at the audience. One of the Playboys even exceeded his bandleader's hope when he smiled real big at a pretty woman on the dance floor. And, she smiled back—real big.

Suddenly, the smiling band member's jealous and suspicious wife jumped the pretty woman and slapped her across the face. The two fell into a walloping wrestling match on the floor. Tables tipped. Beer bottles shattered. Men screamed; women cussed; pandemonium rollicked. Bob Wills stopped the music, tapped out another beat, and the tune of "Faded Love" floated out over the dance floor.

When finally separated from the jealous wife, the pretty—and wrongly suspected—woman just wondered why.

~~~

Now to another century, another genre:

The greatest symphony he ever wrote, he never heard. The conductor laid down the baton at the end of the last movement, afraid to look at the audience. A friend approached the podium and turned Ludwig van Beethoven towards the audience so the now-deaf composer could see people standing, clapping, and cheering for his Ninth, last, and greatest symphony.

~~~

When Arthur Fiedler conducted the Boston Pops, "Stars and Stripes Forever" became the orchestra's signature song. The whole country mourned the popular conductor's death in 1979. At the first concert after Fiedler's death, no one took the podium. The members of the orchestra lifted their instruments. The concertmaster tapped out a beat and then with the podium empty, the orchestra played "Stars and Stripes Forever."

~~~

YOUR CHOICE

History reports:

Giacomo Puccini, the great Italian composer, died before completing his opera "Turandot." One of his students finished the final scene and Arturo Toscanini conducted the opera's premiere performance. When Toscanini reached the last note Puccini wrote, he stopped the music, set down his baton, and declared

"Here Death triumphed over Art." Then he walked off the stage in silence.

OR

The story is told:

Giacomo Puccini, the great Italian composer, died before completing his opera "Turandot." Auturo Toscanini conducted its premiere after Puccini's death. During the performance, the music suddenly stopped. Toscanini turned, faced the audience, and spoke, "Our great teacher was writing this composition when he died and this is as far as he got." Then, with a flair, Toscanini turned back to the orchestra, lifted his baton into the air, and exclaimed, "But we have finished our master's music!"

~~~

Several years ago, Jackie, some friends, and I went to Turkey, Texas, for Bob Wills Days, the town's annual celebration of its most famous son.

On Saturday night, a dance was held in the old high school gymnasium. Four or five hundred real cowboys and cowgirls crowded the floor, with only about twelve drugstore cowboys and girls present—us included. It was the kind of place and event a good fight could break out without a lot of encouragement. People dancing, people drinking, music playing.

These were young men and young women mainly, I guess, from the surrounding farms and ranches. They were big people, brawny people, basically good people, healthy and strong, but when we glanced out the corners of our eyes, we saw one young man on crutches, his legs dangling and motionless as if paralyzed.

The band played western swing, and western swing is only at its best when it can be danced to. The fiddle sounded. We danced. And then, on the dance floor, we saw this: A big, strong country girl embracing and lifting to her chest a Texas cowboy, moving with him in her arms so his lifeless legs could dance, too.

The Ghost of Fort Washita
October 2010

Fear is a cheap emotion, but I'm not going to tell you there's nothing to be frightened of. If Alfred Packer's cannibalism victims woke up the morning of their deaths humming "Don't Worry, Be Happy," they were mistaken.

Fear can be easily manipulated, though, and is easy to provoke. Often we are made to fear what we should not by those who seek power, money, political gain, or some other benefit. Most of us actually enjoy being scared. That's one reason we're so susceptible to fear's seduction.

We hadn't been at my aunt and uncle's house more than thirty minutes when nine-year old Brittany asked, "Are we going to see Aunt Jane? Are we? Are we?"

"We'll see," Uncle Charley said. "She doesn't come out until midnight, and we've got a lot going on today."

We did. It was a family gathering—a big meal, swimming, a trip to the lake and every thirty minutes or so Brittany asked, "Are we going to see Aunt Jane? Are we? Are we? Please."

That's how my uncle, wife, nieces, cousins, and spouses ended up at Fort Washita a little after midnight on a full moon summer night.

Fort Washita was established in 1842 in what is now Bryan County in southeastern Oklahoma. Soldiers in the Mexican War stayed here on their way to the front lines. The Confederate Army occupied the fort during the War Between the States. The fort was abandoned shortly after. Today it consists of ruins, a reconstructed barracks, and the foundations where official buildings once stood.

On this blue velvet summer night, you could almost see the ghosts of sentries standing guard on the barracks' balcony.

Uncle Charley led us past and through the ruins towards the woods.

"Are we going to see Aunt Jane?" Brittany asked.

"It's a full moon and it's after midnight," he replied. "We probably will or hear her at least."

We stopped at the post's ancient cemetery. A marker read "Unknown Confederate Dead."

Uncle Charley pointed to a grave. "This is where Aunt Jane was buried. There used to be a marker, but it's gone now."

A rattle stirred the trees on the other side of the graveyard.

"She got her head cut off and on nights of the full moon, she wanders in these woods looking for it."

We headed down a path deeper into the forest. There was a noise to our right. Brittany and my other nieces screamed.

"There was a little town called Hatfield down this road," Uncle Charley continued, "where people who worked at the fort lived. Aunt Jane and her husband had a business there."

There was more noise back in the trees and more shrieking from my frightened nieces.

"Aunt Jane fell in love with a soldier at the fort. Her husband found out about it and cut her head off. It was never found."

A breeze blew, leaves rattled, and a quilt of moonlight shimmered on the trail. We hiked further and the trail opened up to a big, dank puddle of water.

"He may have dropped it into this spring," Uncle Charley said. "No one knows, but people have seen her. It sure sounds like she's around here tonight." Brittany held my wife's hand and shivered despite the night's heat.

"We may see her yet."

We turned around and headed through the gnarly woods to leave. A cousin's husband joined us as we got near our car. I hadn't notice he'd dropped out of the group about the time we got to the cemetery and heard the first noise back in the trees.

If Aunt Jane wandered those woods that night, we never knew.

"What did you think, Brittany?" I asked.

"It was all right," she said, "but it wasn't as scary as the first time."

Marching On
November 2011

Before each home football game, the University of Georgia Redcoat Marching Band plays "The Battle Hymn of the Bulldog Nation."

You would recognize it as "The Battle Hymn of the Republic."

If you were a Union soldier from Massachusetts in 1861, you'd recognize the tune as "John Brown's Body," a song young Northern boys sang as they went to battle against their Southern counterparts. "John Brown's Body" memorialized the ardent abolitionist who, believing he was on a mission from God, led a violent insurrection against slavery and was subsequently hanged for so doing.

The words to "John Brown's Body" went like this:

John Brown's body lies a-mouldering in his grave,
John Brown's body lies a-mouldering in his grave,
John Brown's body lies a-mouldering in his grave, but
His soul goes marching on.
Glory, Glory, Hallelujah!

Other verses repeat these phrases:

John Brown died that the slaves might be free...
He's gone to be a soldier in the Army of the Lord...
The stars above in Heaven now are kindly smiling down...
His soul goes marching on...
Glory, Glory, Hallelujah!

Poet Julia Ward Howe heard Union soldiers chant this song as they bivouacked near Washington, D.C. at the start of the war in 1861. Her companion, the Reverend James Freeman Clark, encouraged the middle-aged woman to write "better" words for the battle march. That night Ms. Howe had a Divine inspiration, she said, and in one sitting, wrote "The Battle Hymn of Republic."

The words are better, but they express the same sentiment:

Mine eyes have seen the glory of the coming of the Lord,
He is trampling out the vintage where the grapes of wrath are stored,
He has loosed the fateful lightning of his terrible swift sword,
His truth is marching on,
Glory, Glory, Hallelujah!

Before long, Yankee troops sang "The Battle Hymn of the Republic" as they went into bloody battle against their Confederate brethren.

This year our country remembers the 150th anniversary of the beginning of the War Between the States. We watch television specials and read features about that time of our history. Sometimes we hear radio reporters talk about those times long ago. We hear the music of sad violins and see grainy black and white pictures of soldiers and battle. Romantic tales of gallantry and loss are repeated and passed on.

The truth is the War of the Southern Rebellion constituted the biggest political failure in our nation's history. By 1900, slavery had been abolished in almost every developed country, but of all the many nations that ended the practice, only the United States went to war over it. This was a devastating war that set citizens against fellow citizens; a war that left well over a half million people dead, and tens of millions more impoverished, maimed, and disabled. By any impartial standard, the Civil War was an epic tragedy.

The slaves were set free, but was slaughtering each other the only way to make that happen?

Today, the University of Georgia Redcoat Marching Band plays the song Union soldiers sang as they went into bloody battle to kill young men from Georgia. Whether it's winning a football game for the Bulldog Nation or trampling out the vintage where the grapes of wrath are stored, we all still want to be, I suppose, a part of something bigger than ourselves.

John Brown's soul goes marching on.

Jigsaw Puzzles or Sandcastles
February 6, 2005

Petar Dinaric knew the real reason the reign of Pope John Paul I lasted only four weeks.

"Once-a we had a popa who was a woman. Yeaah? But nobody know he wasa a woman until she died. Soa now, whena the cardinals electa a pope—ete's in private—before the smokes comes outa the chimney to announcea the new popa, alla the cardinals feela the crotch of the new popa to make sure he is a man. Well, the excitement was too much for John Paul, he have heart attack and die! YEEEAAAHHH!"

I had never heard the legend of John Anglicus, the female Pope, nor had I ever had a Yugoslav apartment mate. It was 1978. John Paul II had just been elected Pope and I had just met Petar Dinaric. We shared a two-room apartment with two other undergraduate men at the University of Southern California. His explanation for the untimely demise of John Paul I followed his asking me whether I was Catholic.

Petar continued. "I likea the new Popa. He smiles. Yeaah?"

My new apartment mate stood a little over six foot tall, willowy and lean. He had sad hazel eyes, a big nose, and shaggy dishwater brown hair. His skin was paraffin white with big blotches of pimples. Some days he looked like a lanky, hairless beagle.

I made the mistake of asking him whether he was a Communist. Tito still ruled the east European country.

"I ama not a Communist!" His voice rose into fluster. "Why do everyone here thenk everyone in Yugoslavia a Communist? Being a Communist there is likea what? Being a Republican here? Yeeah. I ama not a Communist."

Others would ask him the same question and his voice would get louder and more flustered each time. Not being a Communist was even more important to Petar than even his own Catholicism and the new Slavic pope.

Petar had come to America to go to college. He had no family here, and our apartment was his first home away from his native land. He loved his new place in the world and everything about it. He loved life and its promise more than anything.

"Budallah!" he said. "Howa do you say it in American?" He paused. A few weeks had passed. I had helped him with his English and he taught me a few phrases in Serbo-Croatian. None appropriate for a state dinner, but I could probably now get by in any longshoremen's bar in Dubrovnik.

"I know word for it! Idiot! Jahrhead! Complete idiot jahrhead! Yeeaah! That's whata budallah means! Complete and total jahrhead!"

If Petar ever studied, I never saw him do so, perhaps because American television fascinated him so much. Every afternoon he watched the KABC combo of The Dating Game followed by The Gong Show. He laughed until he cried. He coached the contestants, heckled the judges, and protested decisions. He rolled on the couch with delight as the hour went by.

That semester, a wonderfully exotic French Canadian woman sat across the aisle from me in Professor Larue's class. Her accent was seductive, and her style mysterious. As I walked back home from class one day, I decided I'd ask her out for a cup of coffee after our next class together. Definitely. When I walked into the apartment, I heard the television turned up loud, The Dating Game's MC's banter, and Petar in hysterics.

"Markich! Come here! Right away!" he called, laughing and crying. "This bachelorette is complete jahrhead." He laughed louder. "She keeps getting Bachelor Number One confuseda witha Bachelor Number Two and she'sa completely forgotten Bachelor Number Three! I can'ta believe it! A complete and total budallah! YEEEAAAH!"

I walked into the living room and saw my exotic French-Canadian on the television screen. Somehow I never got around to asking her out for a cup of coffee. Perhaps it was because she confessed to me she hadn't gone on the show wanting a date; she was an actress and wanted the exposure a television appearance would bring. Perhaps it was because I didn't want to be seen in public with a complete and total budallah.

One day I came back to our apartment and all the furniture in the living room had been pushed against the walls. The twilight sun reflected off the downtown LA skyline through our fourteenth floor picture window and the stereo played "The Blue Danube." Gracefully in his arms, Petar held a woman who lived down the hall, gently teaching her to waltz. Before long, every woman who lived on our floor came to our living room for Petar's kind dance lessons. He loved women, and they loved him.

"Markich, doa you knowa Little Debbie who leves in the corner apartment?" he asked one day.

I nodded. Almost every guy who lived in the building knew or wanted to know bosomy Little Debbie.

"Today, I teacha Little Debbie howa to dance and she vas vearing the smallest t-shirt I havea ever seen in my whole life. YEEEAAAH!"

The four of us who lived in that apartment didn't keep track of each other. If one of us had disappeared for a week or so, I suppose we would have noticed, but if one of us was gone, most of the time we didn't ask where.

One Thursday night, Petar disappeared and didn't show up again until Sunday evening. When he got back, he announced he had been to Las Vegas. I knew what that meant: He had gotten home with less than a cent for every dollar he had taken since he lacked the brutal competitive edge necessary to be a successful gambler.

"How did it go?" I asked.

"I had vonderful time!" he exclaimed. "A vonderful, vonderful time! I taught the ladies of the evening new tricks. YEEEAAAH!"

At first, I doubted, but then I remembered how all the women had come to our apartment to learn to dance. Maybe he had. Maybe he had.

Petar soon thereafter joined the USC Ballroom Dancing Team. On the dance floor, the goofy Yugoslav transformed into an East European prince. He was the team's greatest, most elegant dancer. Sometimes the two of us would talk about home and our families. Petar's eyes would fill with tears and his voice with sadness.

"Markich, I have sad news," he told me one day. "My friend Tim. He just break up with his girlfriend. He get kicked out of his apartment. He do lousy in classes. He needs a roommate. He needs a friend. I'm going to move in with him."

Petar packed up his stuff, took his passion for life, and left. I haven't seen him since, but through the 1990's, every news report of the slaughter in the former Yugoslavia worried me. Was my friend and his family, safe?

I wonder now what happened to the passion my generation had decades ago. It seems that most of my friends my age (me included) are ill-tempered and easily agitated. My acupuncturist tells me our livers carry more toxins as we age which upsets our heart meridian which comes out as anger. When I told a client I thought her angry middle-aged son was going through a stage, she rolled her eyes. I'm sure she thought that kind of thing was over when he got through puberty.

Actually, I think we have the same passion, but it is expressed differently. When we are young, we build castles five feet tall with minarets and columns all in the sand knowing the castles will only stand until the tide comes in. Now we put our passion into putting together jigsaw puzzles somebody else made. We get angry and scared when the pieces don't fit or when some are missing, never to be found, or when some are just mysteriously yanked away from us.

I represent some private investigators. Late one afternoon a few years ago, one sought some legal advice. I gave him my best shot. He asked about the fee. I slid across my desk an outdated address I had found on the Internet for a Petar Dinaric.

"There's no fee. Just see if you can find him."

At 8:40 the next morning, the investigator called. "I think I've found your man." He gave me Petar's date of birth, Social Security number, the name of his employer, the employer's phone number, and an address and phone number for his home in San Luis Obispo, California. "He works as a college advisor."

I wrote and mailed this letter:

"Dear Mr. Dinaric,

In the late 1970's, I had a roommate at the University of Southern California named Petar Dinaric. If you are not that Petar Dinaric, please disregard this letter and accept my apologies for bothering you. If you are that same Petar Dinaric, please know that I have hoped and prayed for your safety and the safety of your family as I've heard the news from the former Yugoslavia. I have good memories of you and hope you are doing well.

Yours very truly... "

Several weeks later, I got home from work and sat down at my computer to write. It was telemarketers' hour, and the phone rang. I went to get it to tell whoever was selling whatever to take me off their call list, to leave me alone forever, and to curse God and die. I picked up the receiver.

"Markich! I'm fine! YEEEAAAHHH!"

It was Petar.

"I've been hearing all the news," I said, "and I've just been concerned. I didn't know if you were here or if you had gone back to Yugoslavia or what."

"I'm fine, and my family is all safe. Thank you so much for writing. When I got the letter, I had to call you."

"I don't remember if you are a Serb or a Croat."

"I'm both. My mother is a Serb and my father is a Croat. It makes for a very deffecult situation. When I go to see them, I have to meet them out of the country. It is too dangerous otherwise. It is a very sad situation. Very sad."

"I'm sorry. I didn't know if you'd even remember me."

"How could I ever forget Markich from Oklahoma?"

"You moved out, and we never saw or talked with each other again."

"I know, I know. I didn't finish college at USC. On the dance team, I met this blue-eyed blonde. Beautiful, very beautiful. A Mormon from Brigham Young. I meet her at dance competition. I became a Mormon and we got married. I finished college in Salt Lake City, but that didn't last. No. I had to go back to Yugoslavia to serve in the military for three years. That was how I got to come to school in United States in the first place. This was before all the fighting broke out."

Petar had then returned to the United States and resettled in California. He told me about his job, his new wife, their new baby. We laughed and reminisced. As we spoke, I recognized it in his voice once more.

"Guess what, Markich? My new wife. She is Zen Buddhist. YEEEAAAHHH!"

A passion for life. Always.

Not Yet
May 2010

In the summer of 1965, my parents packed up their Pontiac Bonneville, lassoed their three grade school aged children into the backseat, and took us on a family vacation to California. We saw the Grand Canyon, went to Disneyland, saw the ocean for the first time, and spent valued time with my California grandparents. On our journey back, we took a side trip through the Navajo Reservation and then got back on U.S. 66 towards Oklahoma.

The traffic slowed on the outskirts of Gallup, New Mexico. As we inched forward, we saw why. There had been a horrible car wreck. Eight or ten bodies lay dead on the shoulder.

I haven't liked Gallup, New Mexico since. It's a dusty town, hot, gray, and dreary. Even after a good rain it feels like a miserable place to be.

Later I went to college in California. When I traveled to Los Angeles from Oklahoma, I was going to the land of perpetual sunshine, beaches, movie stars, beautiful women, and fun. When I traveled back to Oklahoma, I was going home to that place of comfort, of good cooking, of familiarity, of unconditional acceptance.

In those days, Interstate 40 hadn't bypassed all the towns between Oklahoma and the West coast. The highway went through the business district of Gallup and the traffic always seemed to just creep through. I never wanted to stop. I wanted to keep on going.

When you reach Gallup going west, there are still hundreds of miles of desert between you and the comfortable blue Pacific Ocean. When you reach Gallup going east, there are still hundreds of miles between you and home. You are just about exactly halfway between one or the other.

Sometimes life feels like driving through Gallup. We are neither at our place of origin nor have we reached our destiny. Our days creep along. It's barren, hot, and dry.

Maybe it is the memory of the bodies by the side of the road, maybe it is that purgatory feel of being halfway there, but Gallup has never been a place I want to be. But, you know, if I ever stopped and spent some time there, I bet I would like the people. I'd find some good restaurants. Before long, I'd make friends. Gallup could become as comfortable as home and just on the outskirts of town, I'd find desert lands as beautiful as any that can be seen.

Vacation and the Smell of Grandmother's Cellars
June 2003

My wife and I stood outside an iron door which, when opened, allowed a cool frosty mist to escape from the earth. Skinny hickory and gnarly oak trees hung over the stairs leading down where we waited with one hundred and eighteen other people to take a four and a half hour hike through a tiny portion of Mammoth Cave. A tour long enough to justify the trip from Oklahoma and safe enough to carry no warnings except of fatigue.

We had driven by vacant black tobacco barns, a red brick church with no name, and the Little Hope Cemetery to get to this place. Despite the shade, the July sun was too bright and too hot. Our middle-class spelunking had been delayed forty-five minutes by darkness.

Once the electrician uncrossed tangled wires so that light returned to the cave, we rushed down one hundred and eighty-seven stairs. (I didn't count; someone else must have, or guessed.)

The cavern's moist air cooled; and the lights subdued, but we rushed.

At our first stop, the National Park Service guide informed us another group would follow in five minutes, and we needed to make up lost time. We did. At the halfway point, our watches confirmed that about half our allotted time had passed. I thought, hoped, the second half of the trip would be slower.

Instead, we strode through long, brown caverns carved from the rock by subterranean rivers. We glanced up ringed holes several stories high and down black holes where the waters continued their slow etching of newer and deeper caves. We paused just enough to take a photograph where calcite rose buds papered the walls. We bobbed up, down, and around gray rock split from other gray rock as crevices. We marched up cave mountains without seeing their grandeur. The air was cold, but we didn't feel it. Not really.

The guides for this tour come in pairs: One to lead and the other to bring up the rear. When the hike began, the leader—she could have been a deputy sheriff or a Rhodes scholar—recommended that the slow walkers start at the front of the line and the fast walkers begin at the end.

My wife and I tested the wisdom of this instruction: After a rest break, we started with the leading guide. Another time, we started at the end, and another, at the middle. Regardless of where we began, we trailed at the end. We wanted to see; we wanted to experience.

The hike demonstrated the immensity of the three hundred and eighty-nine mile long cave, but it hurried by in blurred images.

What was the rush? When would we really get to feel the cool, peaceful air? When would we really get to smell the stale breath of the hidden world? When would we pause to appreciate the awful patience of the creating earth and the power that comes from the waters in the darkness?

Towards the end of the tour, we stopped for the Mammoth Cave trademark experience of total darkness one hundred and sixty feet below the earth.

The guide spoke:

"One."

We closed our eyes.

"Two."

The lights went out.

"Three."

We opened our eyes to pure black, darkness beyond darkness.

"Now I want us to see what it's like to experience silence," the guide said. "No one speak. It's absolutely silent in here."

No one spoke—for a half second, maybe three-quarters of one.

"You will hear your heart beating," the guide said. "They say if you got lost in the cave, it wouldn't be the darkness that would drive you crazy. It would be the absence of sound." The lights came on, and we rushed on without any of us really hearing the silence.

I walked slowly. It had taken the cave ten million years and me, forty-four, to get here. I wanted to show it respect. I wanted to walk in awe.

What was the rush? What were we afraid to hear?

We finished the tour five minutes ahead of time. I then sat in the bright sun and felt its enlivening heat, knowing now with surety that without darkness, there is no light; without the cold, there is no warmth; and without the silence, there is no sound.

Later that day, my wife and I traveled to Glasgow, Kentucky to find ointment for her sore foot. At the Giant K-Mart, there may have been hundreds of people. Certainly down the street at the Walmart Supercenter there were. Either could have been in any community in the country without any change. The tabloids blasted the predictable unpredictable headlines: "I Was a Sex Slave for..." "Bill Leaves Hillary for Another Man." Computerized music, voices, and the sounds of mindless commerce mixed to indistinguishable din.

Why had we been in such a hurry? And, what had we wanted to hear?

This?

Wayne's World
January 19, 2011

Wayne worked in the factory where I did one summer. Wayne wasn't handsome. He wasn't rich. He had a nice, but not a hot, car. He wasn't a big guy and wasn't a little guy. In almost every respect, Wayne was ordinary.

Women loved Wayne.

When he walked in to punch the clock, the country girls who worked in packaging would giggle and say, "Hi Wayne!" The middle-aged women who wore white tennis shoes and too much hairspray would tease him. At break, the prettiest females who worked in the plant would hand him notes and tell him secrets by the exchange of glances.

Wayne had a good sense of humor, but I don't remember anything funny he said. He wasn't a great conversationalist either.

What was his appeal?

I asked him what he attributed it to, expecting him to say his charm, prowess, or a secret extravagance, but he didn't.

"I always have time," Wayne responded.

That was it. He always listened. He never rushed anyone, and he always had the time another person wanted or needed. That's what he said.

Two Harvard social psychologists, Matthew Killingsworth and Daniel Gilbert, recently published the results of a large-scale study regarding the use of time and enjoyment of life. The researchers found that forty-seven per-cent of people are thinking about things other than what they are doing.

Dr. Gilbert says, "I find it kind of weird now to look down a crowded street and realize that half the people aren't really there."

Killingsworth and Gilbert learned that people who focus on their singular tasks are significantly happier than those who are distracted. The evidence suggests mind-wandering causes unhappiness, not that unhappiness causes mind-wandering.

The scholars gathered their data from an iPhone app called "trackyourhappiness" that contacted people around the world at random to ask how they were feeling, what they were doing, and what they were thinking. Approximately 2,200 people participated in the study and over a quarter million responses were gathered. Those engaging in sex reported the greatest joy, with those participating in exercise and conversation the next most focused.

Wayne's secret was that he was always present, not distracted by the past, not distracted by the future. He always had time. Of course, in those past days, the only social media he had were the telephone, the letter, and himself.

No cell phones.

No email.

No texting.

No Facebook.

I wonder how he would fare today.

It's Spreading!
2004

In high school, my friend, Julie, and I started a venereal disease epidemic. Virginally. Without even touching.

It was 1973. Streaking—running from one place to another without clothes except for a ski mask perhaps and tennis shoes—was the greatest, latest fad.

A rumor had spread through my school that the student council president—me—was going to streak the halls at the beginning of the last class period. Students and teachers huddled at their doors to watch. I did, too. Although I had no intention of displaying my shortcomings to the world, I wanted to see who might be imitating me and whether I should be flattered.

No one ran.

Julie and I shared a locker. After the streaking nonevent, we talked about how quickly rumors spread. One of us (I don't remember whom) had an idea. The conversation went something like this:

"Let's each tell one person, and only one person, something completely made up, and let's see how quickly it gets back to us."

"I've got it. Let's both tell one person each there is a VD epidemic here at the high school, and even better, intimate this is a big secret so it should be kept quiet."

That's what we did. Julie told one person. I told one person.

Within twenty-four hours, a massive VD epidemic had spread at our school.

All fiction, as far as we knew.

We live in a world of words, a world of fiction. Like most writers, I love these little symbols on the page and what can be done with them. Even words, though, are fiction, a form for understanding. Americans seek, for example, to be free of the threat of violence by radical religionists, but we call it "the war on terror."

September 11, 2001 is our generation's Pearl Harbor.

Maybe there is a parallel: Massive destruction and death on American soil. But is it really our generation's defining moment? One sovereign country attacked another at Pearl Harbor. Al Qaeda has no known overt sovereign operations. The Japanese military bombed an American military installation. Al Qaeda civilians killed American civilians. Hirohito was motivated, in part, by his people's need for oil and gas. Money Americans paid for hydrocarbons provided bin Laden a fortune. Our own money financed our own devastation.

Whoever came up with the comparison between Pearl Harbor and 9/11 probably owned Tom Brokaw's book, *The Greatest Generation*, and probably loved the million dollar movie, "Pearl Harbor."

The analogy between the two events is pure fiction, but even if it weren't, should Americans react the same way our parents and grandparents did sixty-odd years ago? Have we not learned a more effective response in that time? We probably have, but the fiction of World War II is familiar and comfortable. The new and the unknown never is.

Life will never be the same after 9/11.

Life is never the same year by year, month by month, week by week, day by day, minute by minute, second by second. How functional is this fiction? It is a belief we lived in the Garden of Eden before the attack and a belief in the release of demons afterward. We act, though, as if we are trying to freeze ourselves into a pre-9/11 world, safe from hijacked planes turned into weapons of death.

But wait! Maybe these two fictions created their own realities. Bin Laden and his gang didn't create the appearance of a massive, fascist military force as Germany and Japan had in World War II. Saddam Hussein, in bin Laden's place, became the biggest cur since Adolph Hitler, and his military the most recent and threatening goose-steppers. The tearing down of Saddam's statute in Baghdad was the lifting of Old Glory at Iwo Jima in reverse. Even Saddam's hidey-hole bore a spooky resemblance to the Fuhrer's death bunker.

But, life did change after 9/11. Massive dollars transferred to the military and their contractors. Thousands of young Americans have died or been maimed. Our public life is one of fortresses. Safety has trumped liberty. Fear has trumped hope. Control has trumped freedom.

So, maybe fiction, even inaccurate fiction, creates its own reality.

My yoga teacher went to see "What the #$%&*" Do We Know?" twice and recommended all in her class see it because demonstrated everything she tries to teach. My recently retired Protestant pastor recommended the film to me, and he went to see it twice. After I watched the movie, I thought, "I need to see this again." I haven't. Not yet.

The makers of this extraordinary film overwhelm viewers with new ideas, challenging concepts, and different ways to look at the world. If I understood "What the @#$%&* Do We Know?", the writers and producers seek primarily to show us there is no boundary between consciousness and reality, that each of us creates our own world, our own reality.

Common sense confirms this truth. Most of us know people who are perpetually happy and others who are eternally pessimistic. Some people can enter a scene of crisis and bring peace and tranquility by their mere presence. A lot of parties don't start to get fun until "the life of the party" shows up even if that person makes no remarkable entrance.

A recent study done of Tibetan monks also confirms this truth through the use of a brain scanning process called functional magnetic resonance imaging. Neuroscientist Richard Davidson of the University of Wisconsin, Madison compared the brain activity in Tibetan monks who have spent over ten thousand hours in compassion meditation to the brain activity of novice monks. The testing showed dramatic increases of gamma wave activity in the brains of the experienced meditators. Likewise, the activity there was overwhelming present in the brain's left cerebral cortex, believed to be the center of positive emotions such as happiness and peace, as compared to the more front right-sided activity in the brains of the beginning monks. (See "Scans of Monks' Brains Show Meditation Alters Structure, Functioning" in *The Wall Street Journal*, November 5, 2004, pg. B1.)

Many of the great saints and seers—Lao-Tzu, Saint Francis of Assisi, Rumi, Crazy Horse, for example—created their own realities in a sense. But, how does one do this? Through words? How do you get there?

There are realities beyond words so complex so as to be unfathomable. What do dogs hear when they perk up their ears when all humans hear is silence? What else might be communicating in the unknown silence? How can birds migrate and find their way from the Arctic Circle to the very same tropical nests where they were hatched only the year before? How can a parent intuitively know when a child is in distress half a continent away?

Words and fiction are always shabby symbols of more fascinating realities. The riddle of a Zen koan is an invitation into the realities beyond words.

The great spiritualists have always lived in these places of consciousness beyond the forms of words and fiction and somehow pull from them new realities. That may be the most powerful attraction of the great mystics, but attempts to understand them only through the fiction of words usually fail. Maybe "What the @#$%&* Do We Know?" means that by eliminating the barrier between our consciousness and reality we reach a greater consciousness that allows us to create our own realities. Maybe that is the secret of the great spiritual sojourners.

I am always hesitant to dismiss reports of miracle workers whether they be of Buddha, Christ, the Baal Shem Tov, or a seventy-two-year-old Sunday School teacher in Wyoming. So much of what may be is inaccessible to me.

Daniel Mark Epstein wrote the definitive biography of Aimee Semple McPherson, a controversial Christian faith healer in early twentieth century America. (*Sister Aimee: The Life of Aimee Semple McPherson*, New York: Harcourt Brace Jovanovic, 1993.) It would have been a writer's coup to definitively prove McPherson was a fraud and phony. Epstein found the opposite. McPherson broke up a Ku Klux Klan uprising in Kansas by her mere presence and words. Many of the claims of healing attributed to her could be empirically verified. Aimee Semple McPherson died of a drug overdose, though, in the midst of financial ruin and sexual scandal.

Why do beautiful spirits seem so often to attract tragedy? Saint John of the Cross suggested the dark night of the soul is a gifted, divine state. Where does that dark night come from if we create our own realities?

It has always troubled me that the three spiritual leaders of nonviolent resistance—Jesus, Gandhi, and Martin Luther King, Jr.—died violent deaths. While I have great faith in their ways, it is only logical to ask why I should follow their paths if physical destruction is the result? Perhaps the realities these great men experienced paradoxically created their mirrored opposites.

Back to high school, 1973. The editors of the school paper discussed, I'm sure, the spreading VD epidemic, but decided not to run the story. Too controversial. The administration was a bit braver. It arranged for the county health department to put on a school-sponsored program about the prevention of sexually transmitted diseases. I have to think that resulted in safer sex among at least some of my classmates, decreasing the likelihood of the spread of venereal disease. The fiction Julie and I created—that there was a VD epidemic at the high school—created its opposite, just as the fictions fueling the war on terrorism and in Iraq are quite probably creating their own opposites, too.

I need to see "What the @#$%&* Do We Know?" again. I know I missed much, and given a chance, I hit superficial rather than deep. I do think I would, in any event, add this caveat to the movie: Beware of the realities you create because you may be creating their opposites, too.

But, what the @#$%& do I know?

The End of Protest
December 2011

My boycott failed. A tree falling in the forest made more noise than my effort, and I needed some new underwear. My sixteen year strike had to end.

My protest began during the summer of 1989. In a public square in a city a half a planet away, young men and women had gathered and demanded their voices be heard. Despite orders of the governing authorities to disperse, more and more people gathered in this public square. The old men who controlled the country's government and economy knew what the protesters wanted. They wanted the rights of free speech, press, and religion. They sought to freely assemble and associate. They sought an end to corrupt government. They wanted a voice.

The young protesters ignored government orders to leave the area, and the old men who ran the country decided to clear the public square. If the old men had publicly justified their decision, they would have said that health and safety required the forcible eviction. That was the justification German officials used to remove Jews from the Warsaw ghettoes. That was the justification Tulsa vigilantes used when they burned the Greenwood District in 1921.

In the dark, early morning hours of June 4, 1989, the People's Liberation Army of China began clearing Tiananmen Square. Hundreds died that day because young protesters demanded the democratic rights our forebears held to be unalienable and endowed by our Creator.

The United States government was silent. No formal diplomatic sanctions were imposed. Chinese leaders suffered no consequences as a result of their brutality.

The first President Bush believed the people of China would gain more by engagement than by confrontation. I decided, though, to not buy anything made in China. My boycott failed, but for years, I knew what I bought at the store did not aid a regime that slaughtered its own young for wanting democratic freedom.

Now twenty-two years after Tiananmen Square, China is our country's biggest creditor. Virtually all our consumer goods are made in China. The old men who govern China are as autocratic as ever. The voices of the young are still not heard. Religious minorities are persecuted. Dissenters are jailed.

Now twenty-two years later, young American women and men gather in public squares in cities across our nation demanding a voice and an end to corrupt government. In the dark hours of the night, though, government officials send in police wearing riot gear to clear the public square. Members of the press are turned away or arrested. College students are dispersed in clouds of pepper spray. Our public officials say the action is necessary for health and safety reasons.

From all those years ago, one indelible image remains from Tiananneman Square:

One man standing in a Peking street stopping a convoy of army tanks by his presence and his courage.

One man.

The drivers of the tanks must not have had any pepper spray.

A Broken Kaleidoscope
January 2001

Two boys used to ride their bicycles around the middle-class neighborhood near my office. One wore a silver-spiked leather collar around his neck; the other wore thick black bands around his wrists and ankles. Heavy metal chains draped their white bodies, and big safety pins stuck through their skin. One had Day-Glo green hair; the other, neon pink.

They cruised with sinister arrogance.

One day I told my wife, "I'd want to commit suicide with a ball peen hammer if I worked hard all day and came home to find my kid acting like a demon who didn't know any better than to dip his head in toxic waste."

Her reply?

"You did the same thing when you were their age; you just did it a different way."

She was right, of course. Back then, we wore our hair so long and tangled ferrets could nest there unnoticed. We wore thrift-store outcasts on occasions where clothes were required at all.

When my wife reminded me of the excess of my youth, she sounded like Rod Serling. Instead of the Twilight Zone though, she welcomed me to the Middle Age Zone, a place unimaginable to me when my hair grew magnificently long and my beat-up clothes hung loose and cool.

The most dreadful thing about entering the Middle Age Zone is not the house payment, finding health insurance, paying college tuition, or even, God forbid, buying an SUV or mini-van. The most dreadful thing is forgetting what it's like to be a teenager.

How can we forget the richness of life then? A first romance is in Technicolor; the first broken heart never quite heals. Life is still being learned in wonder and exasperation. Each experience is powerfully new. We forget the luscious dessert is sweeter then and the gall, more bitter. The songs we listen to now on the golden oldies station are no better than the new ones. They simply remind us of life bigger and more vital than what our lives have become. Does passion have to diminish as we age? Do we just grow numb?

I had a friend once who had bright colored hair, not lime green or neon pink, but that rich combination of shades of reds, browns, and golds we inadequately call red. He had freckles, too. His name was Danny. Tall and gawky, he wore braces on his teeth with rubber bands that pulled too tight and often made his speech a mumble. I first met Danny when I was a junior in high school and he was a sophomore.

Danny lived life with hyperkinetic energy then. He moved quickly, but never gracefully, as if one part of his body could not keep up with another. He never wanted to stay in one place too long, and he spoke so fast a court reporter would find it difficult, if not impossible, to write down all his words. Danny played chess with more energy than most people use playing racquetball.

Danny loved words. He delighted in them. He enjoyed puns. He liked to press language to its ridiculous limits. When he was on the high school newspaper staff, he wrote reams and reams of copy: some of it brilliant, some of it mundane, but all uniquely and creatively his own. When Danny and another classmate became debate partners, they gained a reputation on the high school debate circuit, not for brilliant analysis or logical argument, but as one of the best teen-age comic routines in eastern Oklahoma.

Danny had three friends: Bob Schmidt, James Bailey, and me. Perhaps Danny's brilliance and creativity made him too much of a challenge for others. He had a routine where he would ask a series of small-talk questions and if you answered them all, you ended up saying something ridiculous. Sometimes he mimicked your speech and parroted your thoughts to make you really think about what you were saying. Sometimes Danny would get mad and cross his arms and just not speak. We didn't know why.

After I graduated from high school, I went to California to go to college. Danny had somehow finagled a job on one of the county's weekly newspapers as a reporter. Not only that, he had his own column while he was still a high school student. Later, I heard he had gone to Memphis after his own graduation.

I came home from college for the summers. One of those times, I learned Danny had come back from Memphis for good. He had changed. The energy was gone. The love and flow of words, stopped. His humor and creativity, dulled to nonexistence.

One day, Danny stopped by my house. I invited him in, and we sat down to talk in the living room.

"How have you been doing?" he asked.

"Fine," I replied. "What about you?"

Danny shrugged and shifted awkwardly in the chair. "So what have you been doing this summer? Working?"

Was Danny playing his game of small-talk questions? What ridiculous statement did he intend to lead me to? Maybe the old Danny had returned, but he had struggled even to ask what he had.

"Been working," I said. "Seeing some movies. Playing some basketball. Played the piano a little this summer. What have you been up to?"

"Nothing. Sitting in my room. Thinking."

"About what?"

Danny shrugged. "Things. Have you been doing stuff with Schmidt or Bailey?"

"I see them every once in a while."

The air-conditioner blew cool air through the vents. The dog barked outside. Neither of us spoke. Danny didn't want to talk about himself. I didn't know what to say, didn't know why he had stopped by.

Finally, he spoke. "If I put a gun to my head and pulled the trigger, do you think it would kill me?"

"If it's loaded –" I stopped and sat up in my chair. "Sure it would, Danny. Of course. But nobody would want you to do that. Nobody would. Why do you ask?"

He shrugged. "Just wondered. Just curious. So you think it would kill me?"

"Don't even think about it. Nobody would want you to do that."

I don't remember how the rest of the conversation went that day. Some awkward time passed then Danny left. He later asked Bob Schmidt and James Bailey the same question. The three of us didn't know what we could do for Danny. We knew something had fractured in Memphis, but the new Danny was sullen and difficult company. Maybe bad drugs had messed up his mind. Maybe he had been unspeakably abused. Maybe he had discovered he sexually preferred men more than he did women. I don't know; it made no difference. He was my friend.

I returned to school in California. Eastern Oklahoma, Danny, Schmidt, and Bailey became images and seemed less than reality. Several months passed, and Bob Schmidt called.

"Danny put a gun to his head and pulled the trigger," he said.

Schmidt was a pallbearer. Bailey didn't go to the service at all. I blamed expense and a lack of time not to return, although my parents would have found the money and I could have found time.

Years have passed. I live in Oklahoma now. Schmidt left the state and left no tracks. James Bailey reappears every few years. About five years ago, he said we ought to go find Danny's grave. I agreed, but we didn't.

A week before last Memorial Day, I called Bailey back in our home town. "Let's go find where Danny's buried this weekend," I said.

Bailey agreed.

"Would you call Smith Brothers' Funeral Home?" I asked. "We could spend all day at the City Cemetery and never find the grave. Smith Brothers' probably did the service and they would have a map or something on record that would tell us where the grave is."

Bailey said he would make the call. He telephoned back an hour or two later.

"Smith Brothers' didn't do the service," Bailey said. "But the guy working there remembered Danny. He said, 'That's that boy who shot himself in the head down by the river. It was two or three days before they found him, if I remember right.' He even remembered that Neece Funeral Home handled the service. It's a good thing we didn't go looking in the City Cemetery. The guy at the Smith Brothers' said there are over one hundred and sixty cemeteries in this county alone. Anyway, Danny's buried at Storer Cemetery in Kinta."

Bailey thought Kinta was north of the Red River, directly up from Fort Worth. I thought Kinta was in the deep southeast Oklahoma. We were both wrong. Kinta is in Haskell County about ninety miles west of Fort Smith. We decided to go. If our home county had one hundred and sixty cemeteries, Haskell County had at least that many in even more remote locations. The odds of finding Storer Cemetery were not good; the odds of finding Danny's spot even worse. We had to go anyway.

The next Saturday I picked up James at his mother's house near Lake Tenkiller. We drove the back roads through the too-small-to-be-mountains and the too-big-to-be-hills of eastern Oklahoma. Dense forest shaded winding roads. Another car passed every five or so miles maybe. At one point, the macadam disappeared completely and for miles, the car shook and vibrated as it rolled over flint and mud. Seventy years ago, Pretty Boy Floyd hid out in this part of the country. Five decades before that, Belle Starr did, too. It was easy to see why: You could get lost in these mountain-hills and never find your way out.

We passed the turn-off to Marble City. A dark quarry stood by the side of the road. The land flattened, but the trees remained. James spoke.

"Danny's parents asked me to be a pall bearer and I told them no. I've always felt bad about that. I didn't go to the service either. I wish now I had. I was just being that way then. I'm going to write them a letter and apologize. His parents probably didn't know who else to ask. I don't think Danny had many friends."

"It was you and me and Schmidt. That's all," I said. "I've always felt bad that I didn't do more."

"Well, you were in California. What could you have done?"

"I don't know. I've always thought I might have been able to say something to him that might have changed things, something I could have done."

"We did the best we knew to do," James said. "He was seeing the best psychiatrists in Tulsa. He was taking medication, but it didn't seem to work. They couldn't quite get it adjusted right, and they didn't know as much as they do now. Something happened to him in Memphis."

"Yeah. Something happened."

Groomed fields now spread across the countryside. The buildings of Sallisaw appeared ahead.

"I was living in Tulsa when Danny would come up to see his doctors," James said. "He would stay with us sometimes. We had gotten into trouble with the landlord about parking in our front yard. I had told

Danny not to park there, but the last time, he did and it was muddy. I really got onto him—got mad at him, and he went away in a huff. A few days later, they found him. I've always wondered if maybe if I hadn't gotten mad..."

"We did the best we knew to do," I said.

We drove onto Porum and then into the hills of Haskell County. We didn't speak about Danny. Miles passed and a small sign read "Kinta." It was smaller than a wide spot in the road and bigger than nowhere. A new building hadn't gone up there in the last thirty years.

I stopped the car in front of a gas station/convenience store where the two main streets in Kinta intersected.

"Good idea," Bailey said.

We got out of the car and went into the store. The cold damp refrigerated air smelled of cleaning fluids and bubble gum. Two teenage girls worked behind the counter. One had soft blue eyes, high Choctaw cheekbones, chocolate rich brown hair, and slender curves that looked gentle to touch. If she could get out of here, I thought, she could be in the movies. The other was a fleshy blond who wore a tight athletic-gray T-shirt and a big smile. No wonder we were so crazy about girls when we were their age.

"Can you tell us where Storer Cemetery is?" Bailey asked.

They're teenagers, I thought. They won't know where a cemetery is and even if they do, they won't be able to give us instructions to get us there.

The girl with the chocolate brown hair spoke: "Did you come in on that road out there?"

"Yeah."

"Well, just go up that road until you get to the county line road. Turn right and it's right there."

A short older woman with big beauty-shop curls brought a half-gallon of milk to the counter.

"Ella," the blond girl said, "how do you get to Storer Cemetery?"

The older woman looked at us. "Did you come in on that road out there?"

"Yeah."

"You just go up that road until you see a sign that says 'Latimer County.' There will be a road right there. Turn right. Go a mile and a quarter and you'll see signs. You can't miss it."

We thanked them, left the store, and headed towards the car.

"I can't believe it," I said.

"I can't either," James agreed.

We drove up the road we came into town on until we saw the Latimer County sign. We turned right on the county line road. Green wooded hills arose in front of us. I felt anxious.

"My wife made an arrangement with some ribbons and branches of our yew tree to put on the grave," I said. "It's in the trunk. Don't let me forget it."

"I knew I was forgetting something," James said.

I noticed wild flowers growing at the side of the road. "Let's stop," I said. From vines that wrapped themselves around the fences and the trees, James and I picked delicate pink buds. The thorns made our fingers bleed. There would be fresh flowers for Danny's grave.

A sign further up the road read "Storer" and pointed to the right. I turned the car down that rocky road and into the dark shadows of ancient oak, cottonwood, and sycamore trees. A small white steepled church, eighty, ninety years old or older, stood in a small clearing ahead. A big cemetery spread out up the hill behind the church. The sun shown cathedral light through the tall heavy trees and onto the old gray stones.

"It's huge," I said.

"We have as much time as there is sun," James replied.

I turned the car onto the path into the cemetery. James looked out the window. "Most of these are over a hundred years old. God, some are even older."

"Let's drive until we find the new part. There has to be a new part," I said. "That's our best shot."

I drove a quarter of a mile—probably more—up the path into the cemetery. The stones began to look less weathered and the ground looked recently broken in a place or two. I stopped the car. "Let's try here." We got out.

"I'll go this way," James said, pointing to the south, "and why don't you go that way," pointing to the north.

I looked at three or four monuments then I heard James.

"Here it is!"

Someone had already placed a wreath of orange roses on Danny's grave, a deep titian that virtually matched the color of Danny's hair. Fresh flowers in the vases on the granite marker had begun to wilt. Someone else had remembered.

In one of the old, giant trees, a mockingbird sang. A wisp of a breeze rattled the leaves at the very top. Danny had been buried in a place of beauty, a place of peace. Memory hadn't been buried there, too.

I got my wife's arrangement out of the trunk and placed it on the grave. James took the wilted fresh flowers out of the vases and replaced them with the fragile pink, wild blossoms.

"Danny, we miss you, guy!" James said. He stretched his arms out, palms open, and pleaded: "There was so much to live for. Why couldn't we make you see that? Why couldn't we make you believe it?"

I wept. I looked at the tombstone:

DANIEL DOUGLAS McAULEY, III
1957 –1978

We were so young.

The Great Conundrum
July 2013

I love radio. I love sitting in this claustrophobic studio and speaking into this microphone, knowing my words and the sound of my voice travel to places unseen and people unknown. It reminds me that the radio waves that turn into the best sounds are made by real people earnestly trying to entertain, challenge and inform.

The AM radio in the car I drove in high school picked up only four stations in the rural town where I lived: One played old fogies music like my parents enjoyed, one ran only country and western records, one was the local station, and the last was WLS out of Chicago. The DJs from up north talked about the Loop, the big city, to places I'd never been, but I listened to WLS because it played rock'n'roll.

If I had stayed in my hometown, though, the local station probably would have become the default setting on my radio dial. On the morning program, you could hear news from the most recent school board or garbage authority meeting. The announcer might report updates about the highway being built south of town. He would definitely read the daily school lunch menus. "And for today's desert," he'd intone with barely hidden scorn, "wacky cake." A mid-morning DJ would play hillbilly music too raw even for the big city country music stations, and at noon, listeners heard the daily agriculture report. I never understood what that guy said except that some days pork bellies were up and K.C. red was down. By mid-afternoon, the play list had mellowed. The sound shifted to rock'n'roll and pop with the evening rotation. Then, in the wee hours of early morning, the teenage DJ who thought no one was listening would drop the needle on Iron Butterfly's "In-A-Gadda-Da-Vida" and play all eighteen minutes of it.

You never knew what you might encounter on local radio: The hillbilly gospel song of stark beauty played once and never heard again, the flip side of Doris Day's "Que Sera, Sera," a bizarre guitar solo at midnight. OK, some of it was dreck, but that's the way real life is, sublime and ridiculous. Local radio's sheer randomness would have made it my preferred radio setting.

In the last two decades, however, ownership of radio signals has consolidated. Fewer locally owned or operated stations now exist. The DJ's voice you hear speaking on a Tulsa station may actually be coming from Denver. These new corporate owners all employ sophisticated marketing analysis and computer algorithms to broadcast what listeners say they want to hear. But when these marketing strategies were initially implemented, though, the massive broadcasting companies discovered a paradox: The more the stations played what listeners said they wanted to hear, the greater their ratings fell.

You see, the reason the local station of my youth would garner my attention now is because those who ran it understood, either consciously or sub-consciously, the great conundrum of radio broadcasting and that is: What I think I want to hear may not actually be what I want to hear. And that may be the great conundrum of life: What I think I want may not actually be what I want.

Leaving Home
August 2010

Members of my family don't travel light, and my little sister's move from home to college was no exception.

My mother blamed my father for none of her children wanting to stay in Oklahoma and go to college here. He had attended graduate school in Boston which made him exotic in the rural towns where we often lived growing up. My brother left the state to go to college as I later did. My younger sister, Linda, decided to attend the University of Arkansas in Fayetteville, the nearest major university to our eastern Oklahoma home but still distinctly, and on purpose, out of state.

Children who attend college out of state don't come home for the weekend just because they can. They don't bring their laundry home or just drop in for supper with a few friends. A parent is less likely to have a business meeting nearby or to come up with extra tickets for the big game on Saturday. A state line marks a passage. By the time my sister left for college, my parents knew these things.

We lived in an old red brick two and a half story house on the edge of town in those days. My sister had the east bedroom on the second floor, and she'd come of age here. As the end of summer approached, she packed boxes, a footlocker, suitcases, clothes bags, baskets, and more boxes all to take with her to Fayetteville. Once these were moved out, a few teenage posters would remain on the bedroom walls and a couple of stuffed animals would sit on her bed. The empty room, a reminder my parents' last child had left home.

We got up early that August morning of her departure. My father and I began toting the items from my sister's room downstairs to our 1971 Chevy Impala. This was the most exercise my father had gotten that summer. He is a roly-poly man. Although he worked hard, his jobs never required much physical endurance. He'd wiggle his index finger in each of the four cardinal directions and say he had done his daily exercises. He may be the least athletic person I've ever met.

Once the pine green family Impala was packed up as much as it could be, my father, mother, sister and I squeezed into the car and took the short trip through the rolling hills to Fayetteville. After several wrong turns and misguided detours, we found Pomfret Hall, the multistoried residence hall where my sister would live for several years. Linda checked in and filled out some paper work. We then went to lunch and returned to unload the car and take her stuff to her cubbyhole room on the seventh floor.

In polite language, it was a sultry August day in the foothills of the Ozarks. In impolite language, it was a hot, muggy August day sent from hell to remind us of the benefits of repentance. My father and I unloaded the boxes, the footlocker, the suitcases, the clothes bags, the baskets and the additional boxes and took them one load at a time up the elevator to the seventh floor where my sister and my mother unpacked and made her room as much like home as it could be.

It was late afternoon when we finished. I was tired. My middle-aged father must have been exhausted. My parents kissed my sister goodbye. I gave her a hug, and we left her standing at the doorway of her new home.

My mother, father, and I got into the Impala, but my father didn't start it. He just sat there. I could see beads of sweat on his neck and could hear him breathe.

A few moments passed and then he spoke: "I'd go back up there right now and pack and load it all up again if only she'd come home."

No Room in the Coffee Shop
November 2000

Pink flamingoes on marionette feet wander past the smoked glass of the hotel, and neon reindeer glow purple light. Potted poinsettias perch above slot machines dripping yellow leaves as coins clang against metal.

Children ask "Can Santa find us here?"
> A Jewish comedian punches out a blue-edged
> monologue.

Showgirls in Santa hats sing
> "We Wish You a Merry Christmas!"
> > with bare nippled breasts
> > > smiling at a sad crowd.

Christmas time in Las Vegas.
Overture: Have a Holly, Jolly Christmas!

My wife and I ask our cab driver to tell us the location of the First What-Would-Be-A-Prominent Protestant Church in any other town. He doesn't know. Neither does the dispatcher. A blanket call to the other cab drivers brings no answer. Our cabbie drops us off at the Golden Nugget. When we ask the doorman where the church is, he shrugs. So does the desk clerk. We borrow a phone book.

The church is a block and a half away.

WELCOME TO
FABULOUS
LAS VEGAS, NEVADA

I was becoming ill. Exhaustion had first cursed me mid-afternoon. Too little sleep, too much food, too much tobacco smoke, too much work, and too much of my law practice for the year. Now I felt sick. A conclusion following premise after hollow premise, I suppose. I thought it was fatigue. The exhaustion would become a strange illness that felt worse than the worst hangover.

The Vegas virus?

Later we returned to our hotel on the Strip; the evening over.

The montage of nightclubs, casinos, laser light shows, candles and carols finished until Christmas morning.

I couldn't sleep.

Maybe food would help.

In the dark night of the hotel room, the clock glowed 4:08 am.

I got out of bed.

Chapter One: Sleep in Heavenly Peace

The next place: The hotel coffee shop a few minutes later. Busy, but not crowded, with those young enough to be exuberant in the freedom of night; not old enough yet to know its desolation. Others there—by age and circumstance—did.

I wore three layers of clothes and still shivered. I needed coffee. Anything warm. Anything hot.

Noise pounded,

Coins banged and cascaded,

The electronic screaming of the mad machines,

A digital player piano repeating the same Christmas songs with unerring beat.

(Whoever programmed it liked "Grandma Got Run Over by a Reindeer.")

Monograph: On the Etiology of Rangifer Tarandus-Induced Trauma.

The coffee arrived, but I was still cold. The waiter had learned who I was by checking my room number on the hotel computer, and he called me by name every time he had a chance. The meal arrived fast. I was treated as a luminary—in a Las Vegas hotel coffee shop at four o'clock in the morning.

Was anyone else?

I hadn't dropped more than fifty dollars gambling my entire stay.

Two guys sat behind me and argued sports. An Asian couple ate at a booth nearby. In front of me, someone rested his or her blond hair on his or her arms on a coffee shop Formica table.

About the time the waiter had called me by name once too often and grandma had gotten run over by a reindeer one too many times, the blond someone lurched and stumbled to the booth where the Asian couple sat. The Asian man shook his head. The woman did, too. The blond someone stumbled back and laid his or her head on the table, an empty coffee cup in front. No one called this person by name. No one refilled her coffee cup. People came in and people went out. I finished my meal.

The waiter brought one more warm-up of my fifty-cent cup. It was good. I was almost warm. The food had helped. I enjoyed the coffee, felt better, but the all-night restaurant with its bright lights and shiny surfaces felt stark and cruel.

I looked up. Two men stood at the entrance of the coffee shop: One in the uniform of a security guard, the other in a suit only someone in charge of security at a Las Vegas hotel would wear. They looked and then walked to the table where the blond someone's head lay on bended arms.

A boss and a guard for a drunk detail? Overkill, I thought, particularly when this someone was barely conscious.

The someone came to. A person in sexless clothes and a sexless face. She mumbled, though, with a female voice.

MAN IN THE DEAD-FISH GRAY SUIT:
Did you come into this coffee shop without any money?
(Why ask that? I wondered. She's tanked.)
SOMEONE nods her head in a feeble circle.
MAN IN THE DEAD-FISH GRAY SUIT:
Did you drink the coffee you ordered?
(Why not just take her someplace where she can sober up?)
SOMEONE nods and mumbles.
"Did you order and drink the coffee knowing you didn't have the money to pay for it?"

Then I knew. The security boss, with a witness, had asked all the questions needed to prove a prima facie case of petit larceny—very petty—against the woman. They wanted her to admit to a crime, any crime. If she answered "yes" to this last one, they had her.

I had fifty cents in my pocket and enough time to...

The woman nodded.

"Miss," the man in the suit said, "you're going to have to come with us."

And, I watched. I just watched.

Christmas morning in Las Vegas.

Oh Holy Night!

Dumb Okie
May 2010

Don't call me Okie.

An Ohio-born governor of our state tried to make us believe Okie means "Oklahoma: Key to Industry and Education." It doesn't. Some people use the word as a diminutive, a self-effacing way to refer to one's own lack of pretension and home state. That's better, I suppose, but I still don't like the name. When characters in John Steinbeck's *The Grapes of Wrath* called someone an Okie, it certainly wasn't a term of endearment. It's not what real people meant either.

If one looks at academic studies of ethnic minorities in California, one typically finds a section on the Dust Bowl immigrants of the 1930's. You see, the term "Okie" originated as an ethnic insult of sorts, a slur based on one's place of origin and economic status. At worst, the word "Okie" is a term of belittlement. At best, it means a rural unsophisticate, a rube.

Several years ago, I drove to the University of Iowa for a conference. This trip took place not long after the Oklahoma Turnpike Authority dealt with the lack of public restrooms on Oklahoma turnpikes by placing port-o-potties that looked like outhouses in its rest areas, usually right next to the concrete picnic tables and overflowing trash barrels. When I got to Des Moines, I turned right onto Interstate 80 to get to Iowa City where the University is located.

About halfway there, I needed a break so I stopped at a rest area just outside of the town of Grinnell. The rest area abutted a cornfield, but the grounds had been gently landscaped with pleasant shade trees. You could walk your dog in a place just for that, and the children's playground actually looked fun and safe. Nearby, a nature trail led back into a wooded area if you wanted to stretch your legs and take a walk. The grounds were well-groomed and free of litter.

Next to the playground, a beige post-modern building stood as if it had grown out of the earth just for that place. Inside, computer screens showed the latest weather and helped drivers with travel routes. On the walls hung pictures of important events and people in Iowa's history. The vending machines worked, had a good selection of snacks and soft drinks, and charged a fair price for the items sold. If you had time to read the plaques on the walls, you could learn more than you would want to know about agriculture in Iowa. And, the bathrooms were clean and functional, with running water and flush toilets.

The first event of the conference in Iowa City was a reception—a mingle, eat, chat affair—held to give us an opportunity to get to know the others attending. Not too long into the evening, I met a kindly appearing, well-groomed couple. We exchanged greetings.

"Where are you from?" I asked.

"Grinnell," the man said.

"Grinnell, Iowa? Really?" I said. "You've got the greatest rest area in Grinnell!" The couple looked at me like I was a dumb—

OK, call me an Okie, but that rest stop was pretty nice.

Hanging On In Purgatory
November 2011

On Labor Day, 2011, my father began his tenth year in nursing care. He suffers from a form of Parkinson's Disease. He has no tremor but has the characteristic slow paralysis of the disease and some dementia.

When Dad moved into the first care facility, the United States had not gone to war against Iraq. The revolutionary, but now almost obsolete, iPod had just gone on the market. Most people in Middle America had never heard of Paris Hilton.

My father lived in a nursing home in Bartlesville at the beginning. He has since lived in two in Tulsa. The last one, only minutes away from my home and my office. Yet, the drive to the nursing home never gets shorter. It is always one I had hoped never to make.

For those of you who would say you'd never put your loved one in a nursing home or that you'd never allow yourself to be placed in one, know that sometimes there are truly no other viable options. Be aware, too, that there are flashes of hope even in the nursing homes, our secular versions of purgatory.

~~~

My father stopped walking in late 2002. As his disease progressed and his medication lost its effectiveness, he lost the ability to do anything for himself. He can't feed himself. He can't walk. His paralysis is so severe he can't use a remote control even if he could understand its purpose.

He last called me by name about three years ago. We've had no conversation of any significance since

2002. A good portion of the time, he just stares. Months will pass and he will not speak a word, but then...

I stopped by to see Dad after work one day. He was in bed. By this point in his convalescence, his body had become so frozen he could barely scratch his nose.

"How are you doing, Dad?" I asked as I sat in a chair next to his bed.

"Pretty good," he replied, "except for this health problem I'm having."

~~~

Alzheimer's patients have lived at all three of my father's nursing homes. Show up in business apparel and the odds are that some little old lady will approach and ask how to check out of this hotel. Others express concern about paying the bill.

One such patient, I'll call her Bertie, sat in her wheelchair and spent her waking hours making family plans, loudly and specifically.

"Bob's going to pick up Janie's kids in Bixby," she'd say, for example, "and then bring them to Skiatook. Ann, you'll go to the grocery store right after work. We need some hamburger buns. When Ralph gets here, we'll all go to the lake..." Bertie would go on and on, and I hoped her family life had given her such joy that these fantasies gave her pleasure.

Meals are the most miserable times at these institutions. About a third of the residents can't feed themselves. About a third struggle to feed themselves, and the other third don't like what is served or have no appetite.

One night, I came in to see Dad in the dining room. That evening was no different: a third couldn't eat, a third struggled, and a third didn't want to. Just then, Bertie burst out:

"I know what we do, we all go home and start over tomorrow!"

~~~

Just as my father has gone through periods where he has been completely silent, he has gone through times when he shrieks. Short, loud, persistent yells. When asked why he does that, he has said it's just another way of communicating or he does it "because he can."

I think of this shrieking as an expression of existential outrage. The staff at one nursing home found this habit was so obnoxious they told me Dad would be discharged if he didn't stop.

One evening, I stopped in his room. He was in his wheel chair, agitated and making these short, loud obnoxious shrieks. On the television, choreographed violence played: bombs blowing up, guns going off, people killing each other. That night my father's yelling was worse than it had ever been. If I don't get him to stop, I thought, we may really have to move him.

I turned down the volume on the television and switched channels to find something more peaceful. On the country music station, a show featuring the twenty-five most important events of Shania Twain's life appeared. This would have to be more peaceful, I thought. There will be some singing, maybe some dancing. No loud noises or gratuitous violence.

"Dad, this is a special about Shania Twain. Do you remember her?"

He shook his head.

"She's a country music star, and she's hot."

I sat down next to my father, put my arm around him, and hoped his irrational screaming would end. His shrieking slowed and as the program went on, stopped.

"Number fourteen," the announcer read, "Shania buys a Swiss Chateau!"

We saw pictures of it. Like the other milestone segments, clips of Shania's concerts and music videos played.

Dad mumbled something.

"Pardon?"
He mumbled again.
"What's that Dad?"
"She's hot," he said.

~~~

Dad stopped eating. I didn't blame him. The nursing home food looked mediocre and its smell, worse. He would usually eat breakfast so in the evenings, I took shakes to him from Braum's.

After meals, the staff would move the patients to the area by the nurse's station and from here, the aides would take the patients one by one back to their rooms. After meals, the area was cramped with old people in wheelchairs. This is where I'd usually find Dad when I brought him his shake. Dad could sip his drink through a straw but he couldn't hold the cup. I'd usually feed it to him with a spoon.

"Charlie will be here soon," the white-haired lady next to my father said on one of those nights. She was a slender woman of fragile elegance. Her voice was quiet; it trembled slightly.

I lifted the plastic spoon to my father's mouth.

"Charlie will be here soon, and everything will be all right," the woman recited. "Charlie will be here soon. Charlie will take care of everything. Charlie loves me so much."

I continued feeding my father and the woman continued whispering non-stop. "Charlie will be here soon. Oh, Charlie, please come. I love you. I love you so much. Charlie will take care of everything. Everything will be OK when Charlie gets here."

The tremble in the woman's voice was one of fear, I soon realized. Her words, like an ancient chant or religious plea. Over and over again, not pausing for a minute, all the time Dad drank his shake. When he was finished, I took the empty Braum's paper cup to the trash. A big, gregarious, white-haired man walked into the room and to the woman's wheelchair.

"How are you doing, sweetheart?" he said.

The woman smiled.

Charlie had arrived.

~~~

I had nightmares almost every time I went to visit my father the first few years of his nursing home stay. You worry. You grieve. You steel yourself so you won't weep. You feel so helpless. It's easy to imagine your loved one getting hurt, or being neglected or abused and not being able to stop it. It's easy to feel sorry for one's self, too.

One day of self-pity, I sat with my father alone in the nursing home's dining room as the food service staff picked up the dirty dishes and cleaned the room. My father wasn't shrieking then, but he hadn't wanted to eat and I hadn't blamed him and it all felt unfair and it all felt wrong.

A young Hispanic woman cleared a nearby table. She had clear, black eyes that sparkled and a figure like Esmeralda. She couldn't have been over eighteen or nineteen years old.

"Your father?" she asked in a heavy accent.

I nodded.

"I lost mine several years ago. My mother, too" she said. "You are fortunate you can still share life with your father."

~~~

"Dolly said she would have liked to have known your dad before his illness," my wife said one evening. "She wondered whether you had any recordings of your father's sermons she could listen to."

Dolly was the med tech at the second nursing home where my father lived. She spent time with him three times a day dispensing his medicines. Dolly had seen the plaque on his wall commemorating Dad's fifty years of service as a United Methodist minister. No one could miss the picture of Jesus over his bed either, I suppose. Dolly was around sixty years old and was an east India Indian. She didn't move too fast, but always had a calm, deliberative aura about her.

"I'm sure I've got some around here," I replied.

Over the years, my father would, from time to time, give me tape recordings of his sermons. Sometimes they were listened to; sometimes they were simply thrown in a desk drawer or carelessly pushed aside. Preacher's kids are like that sometimes.

Only two, dusty unlistened to cassettes remained in that desk drawer when I looked. Few people still had cassette players so I decided to listen to the tapes before going to the trouble of converting them to compact disk for Dolly. In truth, the Methodist church had all but abandoned my father once he became incapacitated. My father had dedicated his life to God's work, to speaking words of encouragement to those who hurt, to being with those who were ill or grieving, to endure endless church meetings and the nitpicking of the self-righteous and self-appointed. It didn't seem right that after living his life for others, cruel fate would leave him helpless in a nursing home. When I asked why, I heard platitudes or glib answers. When I visited my father, I was alone. I wanted to listen to the tapes to make sure my father sounded as good as he was, not for their content.

The sermon on the first tape was autobiographical. He told the story of his childhood, his call to the ministry, the important events and people of his life, things I had never known. It was my father's voice, too, the one that went silent in 2002. Affirmative, but painfully vulnerable and astonishingly honest.

"A family of four got into their car one evening," my father spoke as the second sermon began. "A husband, a wife, and their two children. The husband was a hardworking man who provided well for his family. His wife was at the church every time the doors open. By all accounts, these people were pillars of their community, strong in their faith, well respected and loved. A drunk driver crossed the road the evening of that family's journey, and every member of that family was killed in the resulting accident. You have to wonder why. Why did God let something happen like this to a good family?"

My father then explored the problems in ever reaching a satisfactory answer in this realm of existence. He preached no simple solutions and offered no false hope. I heard in his words and his voice, though, a man of faith at true peace with the ineffable nature of unjustifiable suffering. From this recording made in 1986, he provided me a way now, over twenty years later, to get through his endless days of nothingness without losing hope. He, in his own voice, spoke of his own situation.

"So what do you say to one who suffers from unjustifiable tragedy?" he concluded. "If you say it's God's will, you blaspheme for no one can know the will of God. You cannot promise a better tomorrow either, for it may not be. Sometimes the only thing we can say is hang in there. Just hang in there."

Hang in there, Dad. Just hang in there.

Roy's Christmas
December 2004

Roy Robinson liked to ride in the car, even if the car wasn't moving. Roy was my brother-in-law, a man in his sixties. He was born with Down's Syndrome. He had lived in homes for the developmentally and physically disabled since his mother died when he was in his late-fifties and his trips to church meetings, revivals, and visits with relatives and friends in north central Oklahoma stopped.

Riding in the car was Roy's greatest delight. Roy loved the simple things: playing with his rope, or drinking a soda, or going for a ride. The car didn't even have to be going anywhere; just sitting in one made him happy.

A problem developed when Roy lived at the Fairchild Center in Billings, Oklahoma. It is a small community—people don't lock their cars—and the Fairchild Center wasn't a facility that locked its residents up. Folks from town would stop at the convenience store or the co-op nearby, and when they'd come back to their cars, they would find Roy waiting inside, enjoying his imaginary ride and refusing to get out.

"Go to Maramec! Go to Ralston!" he would say. He loved to shake people's hands. He was happy drinking a Coke. "Go to Maramec!"

Having a brother or a son like him isn't easy. Roy wasn't always in good humor. He could get stubborn. He'd get cantankerous and impatient. There wasn't always a way to make him understand, but sometimes I wonder whether he understood a lot more than we suspected.

For Christmas a few years ago, Jackie, my wife, bundled him up for a cold December journey. In the back seat of our car, Roy looked like a small child with white hair. This was his Christmas gift: a ride in the car. Material things didn't mean a whole lot to Roy.

The blacktop road was as smooth as political graft—which is probably how it got built, for there was no traffic for miles—and it led from nowhere to nowhere. Roy looked out the window but didn't smile. He hadn't smiled much since his mother died. I sped the car up as we climbed hills and coasted down to give the feel of a kiddie roller coaster. Roy didn't smile. He didn't speak.

Roy didn't talk like other people, so communication with him was intuitive rather than cognitive. "Go in car" came out "go en caw!" and that was his easiest phrase to understand.

We stopped in Perry and bought Roy a soft drink. Jackie said he had always liked sodas, but Roy didn't smile. He didn't grin. I turned onto the four-lane interstate to start the sojourn back. Maybe a faster speed would make Roy happy. I got the car cruising, but Roy just looked ahead. Maybe some movement would please him. Our five-year-old Taurus sedan became a Camaro with me as the Richard Petty of the grasslands. Roy's demeanor didn't change.

The final highway back to the home should have been marked "Fools Beware!" I slowed the car to twenty-five to miss the potholes and craters left from oversized farm equipment.

"I don't think Roy has had a very good time," I said.

"Sing," Jackie said.

"What?" I dodged to miss a chug hole.

"Sing something he might have heard with Mom."

As the car swerved back and forth across the faded white center line, I sang, "When the roll is called up yonder, when the roll is called up yonder..."And, then, from the back seat, we heard: "Whe do ro es coll up yonda. Ha! Ha! Ha! Ha! Ha! Ha!"

When Roy's parents learned he suffered from Down's Syndrome, they asked, "Why us?" Those of us who knew and loved Roy also asked, "Why us?" Why had we been blessed by this gift? And Roy 's life was a gift.

When his mother died, Roy had to be restrained when the emergency personnel came to the house to take Mrs. Robinson's body away. The family debated what to do about Roy. Should we take him to the funeral? It was decided to take him to the funeral home to see how he would handle it. When Roy walked into the room where his mother lay, he took off his hat, placed it over his heart, whispered a few words as if in prayer, and kissed his mother good-bye. He knew. He knew.

When Roy fell a few years ago and fractured his skull, family members gathered at the hospital in Enid. The strong, unquestioning resolve was: "Doctors, Nurses, just because our brother is different, you don't treat him any other way than you would a patient without his limitations."

Roy could never walk again after that fall. He couldn't drink a Coke. He couldn't play with his rope. The family asked, "Why, oh Lord, why?"

The staff at the Southern Oaks Nursing Home in Pawnee where Roy spent his last years will tell you a Robinson was there almost every day to visit Roy, to make sure he was comfortable, to make sure he was safe, to make sure the staff knew they had to treat him as someone without his limitations, to make sure he knew he was loved. When Roy had any physical problem, the family was there.

It wasn't much of a life Roy lived those last three years. I found myself asking, "God, why did you send someone like Roy into this world?"

I think the answer is that God sent Roy to his family to teach us how to love, but what kind of God would do that—send a person into this world simply to teach us how to love? Then I remembered two thousand years ago a child was born in Bethlehem, and a child and a life were given simply to teach us how to love.

On December 16, 2002, Roy Robinson went home. At first, I thought God sent his fanciest Cadillac, his best limousine with a uniformed chauffeur, a refrigerator full of cold Cokes, and all kinds of pieces of rope in the passenger compartment, but then I knew I was wrong.

On that day, an old, faded, beat-up Chevy Impala stopped at the Pawnee Hospital. Roy 's mother opened the door and said, "Come on, Roy Lee, we're going to Maramec!"

Merry Christmas, Roy.

A Valiant Legacy
February 2014

The year is 1966. May. The place: Taft Junior High School in Oklahoma City. The seventh grade social studies teacher has spent the first two-thirds of the hour talking about Communists. Then she says, "And we have Communists right here in Oklahoma City..." And she lambasts as Communists, a group of ministers who have signed and presented a petition to the local school board demanding that the U.S. Supreme Court ruling prohibiting children from being forced to say government required prayers in public schools be respected.

The filing of the petition made the headlines of the front page of *The Daily Oklahoman*. The Court's ruling had already been demonized by its shorthand summarization as "prohibiting prayer in school." In this Cold War time, when billboards read "Impeach Earl Warren," this act of courage by this small group of ministers constituted for many—the social studies teacher included—not only apostasy but also treason.

At the end of the hour, a seventh grade boy walked to the front of the room, looked the teacher in the eye, and said, "My father signed that petition and he's not a Communist." He turned and left.

The boy's father was reprimanded. He lost his church. His family was uprooted from their home. This father was by no means a radical. He had voted for Richard Nixon in the 1960 presidential election. He worked hard, paid his bills, tried to be a good citizen. He simply believed that compulsory prayer is no prayer at all, that prayers required by the government profane the sacred.

Later in his new residence as his family mourned the loss of familiar surroundings and friends, that father sat in the dark and wondered whether he had done the right thing.

~~~

"The building had just been completed the month before," my friend Dean says. He and I stand on the bottom floor of the Mount Zion Baptist Church in the Greenwood District of Tulsa, Oklahoma. "The church had taken out a loan and then it all went up in flames except this basement. Let me show you something."

Dean leads me into a recessed area and he points to black scars on cement walls. "You can still see where the fires burned. The insurances wouldn't pay because they said it was caused by a riot and they didn't have to. The church members met in this basement for years until they were able to pay off the debt and build another building."

Like other public school students of my generation, I had to take Oklahoma history in eighth grade. My textbook had been silent about this. The most devastating racial violence in American history had taken place within walking distance of where my junior high school teacher taught a saccharine version of my state's past.

That official story also left out the chapter on the Ku Klux Klan's domination of my state in the 1920's. During this decade, the KKK was strong not only in South, but also in the Midwest where it had the largest number of members. It was vigorously anti-African American, anti-Catholic, Anti-Semitic, and anti-immigrant. According to its literature of the day, this secret fraternal order was committed to protecting the "purity of white womanhood" and to organizing "the patriotic sentiment of native-born white, Protestant

Americans for the defense of distinctively American institutions."

The Klan recruited heavily from white Protestant churches and civic orders such as the Freemasons and the Knights of Pythias. Over thirty-five thousand people attended a Klan induction in Oklahoma City in 1922. One year in the 1920's, all five of candidates for Speaker of the Oklahoma House of Representatives were members of the KKK. Church ladies formed auxiliaries to support their husbands' nocturnal commissions and to restore and preserve traditional values and morality.

Klan members, disguised in white robes and hoods as the ghosts of the Confederate dead, abducted and physically punished those whom they believed engaged in public indecency, drug use, immoral behavior, wife beating, bootlegging, and other assorted sins.

In Oklahoma, martial law was declared to stop the Klan's vigilante beatings, whippings, and castrations. In the Tulsa Race Riot of 1921, thirty-five square blocks of the African-American community were destroyed, over 100 people were killed, and an estimated 10,000 were left homeless, the result of white mob violence. The governor who declared martial law was immediately impeached.

~~~

When I wrote a family history for a college class in the 1970's, I asked my living grandmothers and grandfather this question: What was the most significant event of your lifetime?

Each answered: World War I.

Each thought this war had forever corrupted the morals of the country.

My sister, brother, and I these days go through family heirlooms accumulated by my parents and their parents, aunts and uncles, grandparents, and great-grandparents. Many were Masons and members of

Eastern Star. All were devout white Protestant Oklahoma Christians.

I wonder how close I get to touching the robes of the Ku Klux Klan.

~~~

I remember a discussion I had with my grandfather during the latter years of his life. He had come of age in the 1920's and had political ambitions like his father before him. By the time of our talk, Grandpa had suffered a stroke. He didn't get animated much anymore, but when I asked him whether he had any dealings with the KKK, he lurched forward and said, "They were all a bunch of cowards. They tried to get me to join. I told them I wouldn't have anything to do with them."

~~~

The wonderful thing about learning is that you deprive no one else by taking what you learn. The wonderful thing about teaching is that you don't lose what you give away. Teaching is also the only gift you can give that will live on into eternity. Something you teach becomes another's who teaches it to another and to another, and on and on and on.

You see, my grandfather had a son who signed a petition demanding that the Oklahoma City School Board respect the decision of the U.S. Supreme Court prohibiting government-mandated prayer in school. And, that son was a minister, who was reprimanded, who lost his church, whose family was uprooted, who later sat in the dark and wondered whether he had done the right thing. But let me ask you today, would my brother—that seventh grade boy who told his teacher that his father was not a Communist—have had the courage to do so had he not been taught by example?

Acknowledgements

Thanks go to Jackie Darrah, Dan and Susan Case, Frank Christel, Rich Fisher, Casey Morgan, Scott Gregory, Vicky Woodward, Jackie King, Becky Hamby, Bob Jones, Mary Coley, Paula Alfred, Jill Byrne Holien, Jennifer Adolph, Mimi Haig, Andrew Marshall, Tom Connor, Ada Harrington, Cathy Morgan, and my readers for taking the time from their busy lives to read this book.

Some of the writing in this volume has been broadcast on StudioTulsa at Public Radio Tulsa 89.5 FM, has appeared at explanazine.com and xplana.com, and has been published in *The Oklahoma Bar Journal* and *Distinctly Oklahoma*. I greatly appreciate the efforts of my editors and producers.

I knew I had hit the big time when Dr. Mouzon Biggs, Jr., began telling some of my stories from the pulpit to his congregation and television audience at Boston Avenue United Methodist Church, Tulsa, and when, a few years ago, the late Bonn Allred, my Tahlequah High School Creative Writing teacher, took me to one of her PEO Chapter meetings to read a few of my essays. Others have also honored me by their teaching, encouragement, and the sharing of these stories. To all of you, a special thanks.

"Every person is a book," my late grandfather used to say.

About the Author

Mark Darrah is a writer and general civil practice attorney with an emphasis on estate planning, probate and trust representation. He lives in Tulsa, Oklahoma with his wife, Jackie, and their shih tzu, King Chipper the Indomitable.

Mark is the author of published fiction and award-winning essays. His commentaries can be heard on occasion at StudioTulsa on Public Radio Tulsa 89.5 FM.

CPSIA information can be obtained at www.ICGtesting.com
Printed in the USA
BVOW11s0612110915

417244BV00011B/169/P